Until the Eyes Shut

Memories of a machine gunner on the
Eastern Front, 1943–45

Andreas Hartinger

Hartinger, Andreas:
Until the Eyes Shut: Memories of a machine gunner on the Eastern Front, 1943–45
ISBN 978-1-69-726234-6
Cover art by Constantin Eugen Cozma: "The Alsatian and Hans, February 1944"

Translated from the German by Vera Filthaut
Photo credit: All rights are with the author

All rights of distribution, including film, radio and television, photomechanical reproduction, sound carriers of any kind, reprints or reprints in accumulation, and recovery in data processing systems of all kinds are reserved.

© Dr. Andreas Hartinger, Zurich 2019
Contact: UntiltheEyesShut@protonmail.com

On, onward
until the eyes shut …

CONTENTS

Introduction		1
Prologue	A day in January	5
Chapter 1	Childhood and early youth	9
Chapter 2	The making of a soldier	15
Chapter 3	Bridgehead Nikopol	21
Chapter 4	Winter in Ukraine	33
Chapter 5	Race from the Bug to the Dniester	51
Chapter 6	All falling apart in Romania	77
Chapter 7	Unlucky in Hungary	103
Chapter 8	The end is nigh	117
Chapter 9	Woe to the defeated	145
Chapter 10	The end of the beginning	161
Epilogue		166

Grandfather

Lines in his face
Eyes still alert
They tell you stories
From times gone by

Prudent and humble
Sounds his voice
Deprivations and sorrow
A whole life long

Listen and note
The experiences he tells of
Take the fortitude they offer
For your life's path

And when the day dawns
As bitter as it may be
When his life comes to an end
And eternity awaits

Remaining a glow in my heart
Never to be forgotten
Easing my sorrow
Always in my thoughts

(Andreas Hartinger)

INTRODUCTION

The following is the literary attempt to analyze the wartime experiences of my grandfather, Hans Kahr. He was born on a hot summer day in 1925 in East Styria (Austria), and hence he was a young man during WWII. He often spoke about his wartime experiences when I was a little boy. Back then, I was often unable to make head or tail of his stories. His words were too romantically transfigured and not always clearly definable. At least not in a child's mind. It was only with age that I was able to structure and understand his experiences. I do not want to seem to be making a personal judgment about his life; it was simply the case that someone had to put his extraordinary youth and wartime experiences on paper. Grandfather and I finally succeeded in doing so, after hours of painstaking work and emotionally unsettling conversations. His phenomenal memory and the detailed notes he took during and after the war made all the difference.

My grandfather's life was no walk in the park. He was the first and only son in a poor farming family. Their daily life was all sacrifice and hard work. Nonetheless, hyperinflation consumed most of their savings and valuables.

Although the young Republic of Austria had changed its monetary policies, disaster was always closer than the political leadership would have liked. So, in the early '30s, the global economic crisis struck Austria with full force. Unemployment had reached 560,000 by 1933. The manufacturing sector was especially hard hit, with nearly one in two losing their jobs. In agriculture, however, there was at least the possibility of self-sufficiency. National debt rose by a third within a couple of months. Dissatisfaction grew, especially amongst the youth. In February 1934, when this pent-up anger finally offloaded in the form of a fratricidal war, hundreds died. Subsequently, Austria introduced a new authoritarian constitution and a restriction to freedom of action on foreign policies. This, however, led to Austria's further isolation from other European democracies.

For this reason, the dominant experience of an Austrian citizen in the '20s and '30s was that of unemployment. On top of that, it did not take long until the Austrian government was unable to pay sufficient unemployment benefits. So-called "modulation" (being taken off social welfare), which had robbed the populace of any financial support, floated constantly like a hangman's noose over their heads. How were you supposed to feed your family without a source of income? Hunger and frustration, hatred toward the establishment, and a lack of control over one's own destiny were daily themes.

But there was light at the end of the tunnel. Rumor had it that in neighboring Germany a new political party had taken control. One that guaranteed work and food. Longing for a life without hunger and uncertainties, people were susceptible to these promises. That is how a new, sinister chapter began for Austria.

With hindsight, the First World War—which was supposed to "end all wars"—was the root of the next disaster. The heavy burden of the treaty of Versailles was weighing the Germans down. With befitting foresight, the French Field Marshal Foch once said: "This is not a peace treaty, but a twenty-year-long truce."

Indeed, history took its course and would eventually catch up with a young man in a remote corner of the East Styrian hills. And that's when the journey began …

PROLOGUE: A DAY IN JANUARY

I had been at the Eastern Front for a month by this time. A handful of comrades and I had occupied a group nest near the bridgehead of Nikopol. We were all from Ostmark (Nazi name for Austria after the 1938 annexation), all but one Alsatian. The leader of our group was an Oberjäger (NCO) from Styria. He and the Alsatian already had plenty of combat experience, unlike the rest of us. A group nest usually consisted of a fixed shelter and its slit and fire trenches, from which we would fight the enemy. The previous intense battle had left the front line quite thin, and we were defending it in sections rather than in a continuous line. Our most important weapon was our heavy machine gun (MG for short), for which we had meticulously created several camouflaged fire positions.

To prevent unwanted surprises, we would take it in turns to guard our forecourt. Rations and munition were supplied to us under the cover of darkness—a laborious and often dangerous undertaking. Due to the flat terrain, there was a visibility range of several miles. Not just for us of course, but also for the enemy.

The average age of our group was twenty, but we all looked much older. The cold, hunger, fatigue, and constant fighting had taken its toll. If one looked into the sunken eyes of a comrade, there was nothing boyish left in them. All youthful twinkles and innocence had long been exchanged for another ghastly face of humanity. Kill or be killed. Not what any of us wanted, but there was not much choice.

In trench warfare, it is customary to keep the enemy busy with targeted, often bold assaults. And so it happened that one cold January night our base was attacked by a Russian reconnaissance detachment. I had only just been relieved of my guard duty. Back in the bunker, I had taken off my belt, put my semi-automatic carbine in a corner, and was heading to my straw sleeping bag to get some much-deserved sleep. By now I had stopped bothering to take off my boots or my combat jacket. It was freezing, even inside the bunker. Nonetheless, I sunk into a death-like sleep straight away. The front was quiet. Eerily quiet.

Then, suddenly: the sound of flares. These were usually fired to detect suspected enemy movement. Nothing unusual, had it not been for the suppressed alarm call from our young sentry. All of us inside the bunker jumped straight up and raced out, the Oberjäger included. I grabbed my carbine and a full ammunition box in passing. The bright flickering light of the flares showed the ashen face of the young guard. "Oberjäger, movement about 50 meters ahead": that was his brief.

Each MG was manned by two gunners. I was gunner 2. The show started just as gunner 1—the Alsatian—tore the stiff canvas cover off the MG 42. Submachine gun salvos flew by all around. They hit the trench wall behind us like bolts of lightning. There was no time to think. The Alsatian pulled the trigger of our MG, sending our deadly load out into the steppe. The first belt of ammo was soon gone, its continuous staccato echoing through the night. The next belt was inserted in a flash; we were a well-rehearsed team by now. Suddenly, out of the corner of my eye, I saw the Oberjäger stretching out. With a yell—"Grenaaade!"—he threw the very same hard to the right. It landed just short of our position. We instinctively pulled our heads down deep between our shoulders to shelter from the shrapnel.

"Too damn close," I thought. "Is this madman trying to kill us?"

While frozen blocks of earth pelted all around us, we were already back in our positions continuing the firefight. Robbed of the element of surprise and by now also the cover of darkness, the Russians had no other option but to retreat. Angrily firing from all barrels, they returned to their own trenches, disappearing as quietly as they had arrived.

Just to be sure, we remained in our positions for a while longer. Since it was my job as gunner 2 to make sure we had enough ammunition, I made my way back to the bunker. On my way, I bumped into the Oberjäger, who mumbled: "That was close, too damn close."

At first, I did not understand what he meant. Then, at dawn, there he was, in a shallow ditch about 5 meters from our MG: a Red Army soldier, covered in shrapnel, his stiff frozen hand still clutching his Soviet submachine gun with drum magazine (PPSh). Wearing white camouflage dress, he had come dangerously close to our position. His right side was torn apart. There was blood all around him. Judging by the marks in the snow, he had been crawling across the terrain for the last 50 meters or so. Our Oberjäger must have noticed the movement. I dread to think what would have happened if he had not reacted so quickly. Death—or worse: imprisonment in Siberia.

The next night, the Russians visited once again, unnoticed. This time to retrieve their dead comrade. All that was left in the morning was a red patch in the snow …

CHAPTER 1

CHILDHOOD AND EARLY YOUTH

My home was a modest smallholding in the East Styrian hills. It was classed as a "Berglerhof," and had been in the family for generations. "Bergler" was a collective term for the smallholding community that had to find their meager income on those hard-to-farm hilltops. Economically and socially, they were classed as lower peasantry. Judged by the size of their land or their livestock numbers, they were often put on the same level as the "chaste" (part-time farmers or leaseholders) or even classed as simple servants. They were snubbed by the rich farmers of the lower regions. The Bergler showed an especially strong bond to their homeland and to nature, however. They still practiced the old customs and ways of life of this remote borderland.

Our home's birthing room also served as a nursery. Later on, I had to share it as a bedroom with my two sisters. In addition, there was our parents' bedroom, a spartan bathroom, and the kitchen, which was the family's meeting point and social room. The house was made mainly of wood, clay, and straw. It was not until much later that some of the living quarters were built from kiln-fired clay bricks. The roof battens of the cowshed and of the adjacent pigsty were still nailed to the rafters with wooden pegs.

To the north of the farm, a dense wild hedge offered shelter from adverse weather conditions. It bordered the edge of the woods, where it then changed into a simple slatted fence. By this hedge, there was an assortment of fruit trees, lifesavers during the meager winter months. The women would dry the apples, pears, and plums, and store them in little hand-woven baskets in the attic above the kitchen. It was up to us young children to collect the windfall. The men would press the fruit for juice.

Small fields and mountain meadows spread to the south and to the east. The pride of all Bergler, in addition to their strong draft oxen, were the rows of lovingly tended grapevines. Excepting the war years, I was to spend the whole of my life on this farm. Like my father before me.

During WWI, my father had served the monarchy. As a member of the KuK army, he had been severely wounded in the battle at Przemyśl Fortress. Once recovered, he fought the Italians in the battles of the Isonzo. We would often sit together in the kitchen after a hard day's work, and he would tell us about the war—especially about the long, bitterly cold winter months. Stories about daredevil attacks over sharp cliff edges and the many times he had escaped death's embrace by a hair's breadth. I was fascinated by those stories about a completely alien world. They had absolutely nothing in common with our relatively peaceful existence. I listened while holding my head in my hands in anticipation. Again and again, he would draw on his pipe with relish, and then, after some reminiscing pauses, he would blow the smoke toward the ceiling. "Well, well, my dear children," he would say. "Those were bad times, but all is good now."

Then, after a lengthy monologue, he would tap the ashes from his pipe, and we knew it was time for bed. Our mother would already have heated three round stones in the hearth. She would then wrap them in thick layers of cloth and tuck them into our beds down by our little feet. The warmth would quickly spread between the cold sheets and last for hours. When the bitter cold woke me up in the middle of the night, I would use my feet to roll the stone toward my upper body. Once it was within reach, I peeled the freezing cold cloths off it and held it tight against my chest in order to extract the last traces of heat it held. Then I would fall asleep once more, happy and cozy.

Helping with all the chores was normal for us youngsters. With "youngsters" I mean all of us children, from the age of five. All of the land had to be worked by hand. It started in spring with potato planting. Our mother dug the holes, and we dropped the seeds in. In summer, the grain needed to be cut. We would collect the corn sheaves and ears in separate heaps. Harvest soon followed, then threshing, and finally, in autumn, we would collect the windfall. On top of that, there was always something to do in the house or in the stable.

Between 1931 and 1939 I went to elementary school. We would walk to school, me and my sisters. An hour there, an hour back. In all kinds of weather. On a typical day, before setting off, I would take the cows out to graze at five in the morning. If we did have some free time, we would play dodgeball or even play the odd prank. And in winter, of course, we went sledding. The steep slopes to the north and south of our house were just perfect for that.

I look back upon my childhood with fondness. We were carefree and in tune with nature. Life still seemed like a big adventure. Our upbringing was strict and full of hardships. Thinking back, it might even have been dull at times, a consequence of the difficult circumstances. There was ever more strenuous work to be done on the farm. Every little hand was needed to wrestle out of nature the yields we needed to survive. Later, as I got older, I also had to help slaughtering the pigs and chickens. This was always a special occasion, for we did not have meat on the table very often.

But it was precisely this hardship that prepared me for the vast Russian plains and the catastrophic conditions of my captivity. I still see before my eyes weaker comrades lying by the wayside during our miserable retreat, wounded or exhausted, begging for a pistol to put an end to their suffering. I always wanted to save myself from this misery, so I resorted to the teachings and experiences of my childhood.

As carefree as my childhood had been, it was soon to be over. After elementary school, I went to the local farming college from 1939 to 1941. Here, us young farmers were taught everything about agriculture and livestock. Lessons were held once a week. The rest of the week was spent dutifully supporting the farming community. On larger undertakings, such as digging pits or trailing field drains, everybody lent a helping hand. Family members, neighbors, the old and the young. No one had to be encouraged to help. Mutual support was normal, an unwritten rule amongst the Bergler.

Soon after the annexation, youth organizations such as the Hitler Youth (HJ) and the Federation of German Girls (BDM) arose all around Austria. These provided the new rulers with a fresh reservoir of human resources. War was impending, and every able body was needed to achieve the extremely ambitious goals of the new authorities. I started my pre-military training in June 1941, by which time the war in Europe had been ongoing for almost two years. There was an HJ camp in the neighboring village. It consisted of some wooden barracks. We were clothed in military shirts from day one of this three-week training period. There was a duty roster, almost equivalent to an army one, and a daily run to an old castle ruin and back. Since we were all strapping young farmers, we had no issues with any of the physical tasks. We were taught basic military skills and knowledge, such as marching, behavior in the field, orientation, discipline, and comradery. They had also set up an assault course to imitate the movements during battle. (I was not as good as some of the others at firing small-bore rifles, due to a slight visual impairment in my right eye.) Then there was a pond in the middle of the camp. If something had not been to the liking of our superiors—during camp inspection, for instance—they made us jump into it. As punishment, or at least, that was the intention. We thought it was great fun. But that was a closely guarded secret.

One purpose of having us live in barracks was to isolate us from civilian life. One day my father came to visit on his bicycle. They stopped him at the gate. It was only after a serious complaint to the camp commander—stating that, surely, he as a war veteran should be allowed to observe his son's training—that they let him pass. He had brought with him some apples and fresh underwear. At the time, we did not quite understand how serious the situation would become. For us, the HJ was more like a leisure club. None of my class were forced to join the organization, and most of us refrained from doing so. It would have never crossed my mind to be politically active at that age. The camp was just a welcome change to everyday life. Nobody thought about what it could mean to storm the enemy under artillery fire or to take aim at a person whose only desire was to live too. My father knew about it, but little did he know what life had in store for us youngsters.

CHAPTER 2
THE MAKING OF A SOLDIER

In August 1941, shortly after the beginning of the Russian campaign, I and four other young lads from my remote region were called up. I had just turned sixteen. We traveled to Fürstenfeld. Among us was my old school friend Toni, who lived close by. Fate would have it that, while in Russia, we would bump into each other on several occasions. Toni was a sniper in a Jäger platoon of the Gebirgsjäger Regiment 144 (GJR 144); as for myself, I was a machine gunner in the 4th Heavy Company, I. Battalion, Gebirgsjäger Regiment 138 (GJR 138). Both regiments belonged to the 3rd Gebirgsjäger Division (3 GD).

The enlistment procedure itself was organized in the secondary school, a splendid modern building. After being declared fit for duty, we were paraded around town. From then on, every Sunday in church, we would wear a plaited-flower decoration on the lapel of our traditional jacket. Enlistment was followed by an opulent lunch, a small token from the ruling party, paid for by the local mayor. We filled our stomachs and enjoyed a beer for the very first time.

Enlistment marked an important milestone in the life of a young farmer. Still engrossed in Austro-Hungarian traditions, being declared fit for service also meant being capable of taking over the smallholding, becoming a master of the trade you had learned, or getting married. Being declared unfit for service, on the other hand, was as a lifelong stigma. Quite often those young men would leave home and work elsewhere, trying to get through life as peasants or farm workers. This was difficult for those who lacked the special talents to propel themselves out of their misery. On all the tavern tables of this remote borderland, it was still commonly agreed that to serve Kaiser and country and to put one's own life on the line was the highest distinction and simply the greatest adventure of classic Bergler life. Stories of war, major battles, hardships, and distant places were of equal socio-critical importance as the tales of rich harvests and unfortunate weather caprices. This was how every generation passed the quintessence of manhood on to the next. Of course, one was proud of one's own military fitness, and from that moment one glanced contemptuously at those who could not lay claim to this kind of "nobility."

Before we would join the Wehrmacht for frontline duty, however, we had to serve for a few months under the so-called Reichsarbeitsdienst (RAD), or "labor service," donating our labor to the nation. For me, this phase started on January 12, 1943, and lasted until April 9 of the same year. I took the train from Fürstenfeld to Heidelberg in the Rhineland. There, along with two hundred more East Styrians, I enlisted in the RAD camp Neckargerach that very same day.

After receiving our military kit, the suitcases with our personal effects were sent straight back home. Our company consisted of four platoons, with a total workforce of around 250 men. We were also joined by a few Bavarians. There were no cultural or language differences between us, and we got on well from the very beginning. This mutual acceptance certainly strengthened our feeling of belonging to the new Reich.

Our daily routine was similar to the one in the military training camp of the HJ. Straight after sunrise, there would be obligatory morning exercise. Afterward, we would set off by truck to the Siegfried Line to fulfill our labor duties. It had been built as a defense line against the French in the '30s. Following the recent victory over France, these fortifications were no longer needed and had to be dismantled. All reusable materials, such as cables, tank traps, and shelters, could be used elsewhere. The area was full of trenches and steep slopes. Work was hard and exhausting. Toward the end of our RAD deployment, we were sent out to work on some of the large local farms. They were huge in comparison with our smallholding. I have fond memories of this, especially of one farmer, who also owned a local pub. Mainly of his generosity. He always gave me plenty to eat, one day in particular, after planting oats using cows as draft animals.

Altogether this phase was not a bad one. The locals were friendly and showed us enormous respect. There is only one moment that does not bear thinking about. We had to prepare the fields for planting, and in absence of suitable machinery, the whole company was crawling on their knees, digging the stones out of the hard soil by hand. All this was done to gain just one hectare of land. Due to the constant reports of our army's victories, I could not quite understand the point of what we were doing. Had our Wehrmacht not just conquered large areas of the fertile Ukraine? Was the "Lebensraum" in the East not large enough to feed the German Reich?

Well, so be it. During our pre-military training we were also introduced to some new military drills, such us singing while marching and parading with a spade. I liked both from the start, mainly because they usually took place on the picturesque banks of the river Neckar. After this tough but pleasant and eventful time, I spent a few more months on my parents' farm, until in June 1943 I received my call-up papers. My orders stated for me to report to the barracks of Gebirgsjäger Regiment 138 (GJR 138) in Maribor on June 23. This was a training and replacement battalion, whose task it was to provide all reinforcements required to the 3rd Gebirgsjäger Division (3 GD) fighting on the Eastern Front. At that time, the Third Reich had been at war for four years, fighting simultaneously on several fronts. To nourish the beast of war, the sons of 1925 were called to arms from 1943 onward.

Maribor, where I was to be enrolled, was a town of simple beauty full of KuK architecture. Our four-story barrack was also a remnant of the former Austro-Hungarian reign, and more than ready to receive its new recruits. We were allocated to our units by height. This typical Prussian measure ensured that a battalion gave a uniform appearance when on parade. Being one of the smallest, I was allocated to the 8th company. I got on well with the people in my new home. The tone was comradely, but the training would demand a lot from us all.

At this advanced stage of the war, basic training only lasted four months, and it was focused on combat. More formal training—which would include things like drills—was pushed to the back, for the Reich needed fighters, not parade soldiers. On one such occasion, while crossing a bridge over the river Drava, I forgot to salute an officer. I got a dressing-down straight away and was told to report for punishment the next morning. I was an "obedient" soldier, but nature has also equipped me with some shrewdness.

Needless to say, I did not report for punishment the next morning. I decided to wait and see. That morning's class was taught by the very same officer. He mentioned the incident, cautioning us all, and requesting that the culprit report for punishment. I was seated in the first row, right in front of him, but he did not recognize me—so I managed to get away with my misdemeanor.

On another occasion, we were sent to Graz for a medical. There, I stated that I had a visual impairment in my right eye. The duty doctor did not take much notice of this, but he seemed to have me down as a bit of a slacker, which he duly expressed in a letter to my commanding officer. This letter was handed over to me to pass on, though. Suspecting bad results, I opened it on the train back. My suspicions were confirmed, and I thought it best to make the letter disappear. Which I promptly did. No one ever asked for it, but I am sure I saved myself a whole lot of grief.

In the second half of our four months, basic training was completely taken up by combat training. Our only day off was Sunday, when we were allowed to wander around Maribor wearing our best dress. I was trained on the pistol, the 98k carbine, and the MG 42. I was quick in learning the various weapon drills and the other combat techniques. My group commander was an Oberjäger from my neighboring region of Feldbach. He had already gained some experience at the front and tried to prepare us as best he could for what was to come. He was never too strict during our training. Our youthful curiosity made us ask what it was like to be at the front. I must say that he had not been very liberal with the truth. He kept rather silent about the actual severity of fighting against the Russians. Perhaps he simply did not want to take away the illusions that protected us from the harsh reality awaiting us. I soon saw it for myself, though. After the first few days at the Bridgehead of Nikopol, I already knew.

I was allowed home for two weeks at the beginning of September, to help my parents one last time. "Harvest holiday," they called it. Upon my return to the barracks, I brought our often-moody duty sergeant thirty eggs, and from then on I had a better standing with him. As we came to the end of our basic training, partisan danger was often proclaimed. If the alarm was called, we would move into our positions on the outskirts of Maribor. Here, we would dig our shelters under the cover of darkness, and wait. There were never any incidents, however, and I never did set eye on any partisans.

By now we also felt that all of this was getting serious. Before my upcoming deployment, I spent a last holiday at home. My rifle and my kitbag had already been handed to me upon leaving Maribor. My sisters especially showed great admiration for the nice uniform and the shining Edelweiss on my cap. Even my father was evidently proud of my belonging to the mountain troops. As I'd been ordered to, I reported to the Kaiser-Franz-Joseph barracks in Graz on November 27. It was a difficult farewell. My mother and my sisters wept as they gave me one last hug. My father, never losing his equilibrium, shook my hand and mumbled a few encouraging words. From Graz we were moved to the Khevenhüller barracks in Klagenfurt. There we were joined by the 7th and 8th Companies from Maribor. With some other units and some convalescents, we formed a march battalion of around one thousand men. Well-nourished, strong men—some young, some middle-aged. It was a common practice of the Wehrmacht to bring replacements to the front in such form. These march battalions had already been issued with light infantry weapons, in case they ran into trouble on the way. Once at the front, the march battalion was disbanded, and the soldiers distributed to their relevant companies.

In these last cold days of November 1943, I left my homeland to fight for a cause that, in principle, was not mine. But, like many others, I did my duty for the fatherland. As had been the custom for our fathers and forefathers. Eighteen years old and in the prime of my youth, I was about to embark upon a journey from which I would return a marked man.

CHAPTER 3

BRIDGEHEAD NIKOPOL

In Klagenfurt, they crammed us into sparsely equipped freight cars. From there, we made our journey via Hungary and Romania to Odessa, a large port on the Black Sea. Here, the battalion was loaded onto trucks that brought us to the bridgehead at Nikopol. We crossed the river Bug near Nikolayev many hours later using an inflatable bridge. The temperature was just above freezing. It was another 250 kilometers to get to our position on the river Dnieper. We arrived in the town of Nikopol on December 11, 1943, and then we finally crossed this formidable Ukrainian river from west to east.

Just as we arrived, two Fieseler Storch landed on a field nearby. These tiny, featherlight aircraft were constructed especially for short landing strips. Four officers in white lambfur coats disembarked. One of them was the later General Field Marshall Schörner, renowned for his extraordinary staunchness and fearlessness. If this general was in command, then shit would hit the fan. The battalion gathered in formation and the general took in the parade. Then he held a speech that I will remember forever:

"To the young ones: stand to attention! To my old front

fighters: stand at ease! Men, the battle here at the bridgehead will be a tough one. The enemy on the other side is already gathering reinforcements and will attack very soon. Be steadfast and brave for the good of our fatherland. I have always been able to rely on my mountain troops."

As a matter of fact, the manganese mines and smelters in Nikopol were of great strategic importance to the German defense industry, especially for the production of special steels and aluminum alloys. They were refurbished in 1941, immediately after conquest, and just one year later they were providing about 90% of the metal needed by the German war economy.

We moved toward the front in long rows. In ominous darkness. And soon, we sustained our first casualties, mainly from splinters and ricochets. A bitter taste of what was to come. Suddenly, everywhere along the line, flares rose to the sky. Machine guns rattled here and there, grenades struck, and single shots whipped through the air. There was no doubt about it: there was a war being fought, right here, 1,500 kilometers east of my home village. At that time, even the most experienced soldiers among us did not suspect that this distance would slowly melt away over the next few months.

Once we had arrived at our destination, we were assigned to our individual companies. Our headquarters was nestled between two Russian farmhouses. Because of my MG training, I was allocated to the 4th (heavy) Company, Gebirgsjäger Regiment 138. During the night of December 12 to 13, I finally stood on guard for the first time. One of my comrades—the Alsatian—guided me. He showed me the Russian positions and what to pay attention to. He had already been at the front for a year by then and had joined the mountain troops for his love of the mountains. He remarked ironically that he had not yet seen any, but was hopeful that he would, once we advanced toward the Caucasus again.

The terrain was flat. You could see for miles—though sticking your head out above the trench by daylight would have been suicide. The Russian snipers simply fired at everything that moved. The nearest of our own troops were about 100 meters away. In order to be able to support each other against upcoming attacks, the fields of fire of the individual positions always overlapped.

The whole country lay under a fine blanket of snow. The temperature was around -5 °C, accompanied by a sharp easterly wind that went right through us. I was awed by the vast Russian expanse. My East Styrian home was laced with hills and forests, with a farm on every hill and fields all around. But there was nothing dominating the barren landscape here—no shrubs, no trees, no houses. It suddenly occurred to me that the largest river known to me up to that point, the Mur, would probably not even have been honored with a mention on a Russian map. By contrast, the Dnieper, which separated the bridgehead from the hinterland, was over 500 meters wide in several places!

The Russians quickly fulfilled General Schörner's promise. On December 19, 7 a.m., strong artillery preparations commenced against the positions of the 3 GD. I had just fallen asleep when the earth began to shake all around me. The Alsatian woke me up with the words, "Hans, get up, get ready—not long now before you will finally set eyes on your first Russian!"

My heart raced like never before. Every shell impacting nearby pressed snow dust through the sides of the roughly hewn bunker door. We all sat and waited tensely. Only the Oberjäger continued smoking, writing a letter by the pale candlelight. His stoic calm seemed out of place to me, the newcomer. For me, the biggest burden of being at the front has always been the never-ending wait, the condemnation to idleness, watching on while the world around you seems to be drowning. The shelling was so intense that soon it was impossible to distinguish individual shots from each other. The Oberjäger had mentioned earlier that he had experienced worse shelling than this. He anticipated that the enemy would probably try to shoot down our positions before the ground attack. At the time, I could hardly imagine that this inferno could get worse. The Eastern Front, however, taught you a new lesson every time, especially when it came to the acting parties' excessive urge for destruction.

The firing suddenly stopped. We stormed out of the bunker. I ran over to the first MG position with the MG tripod mount strapped to my back and my carbine in my hand. But the emplacement had taken a direct hit and was now useless.

"Change position, on, on!" the Alsatian yelled behind me, giving me a thump in the back. Lugging our heavy equipment, completely out of breath, we reached the alternative fire position just in time. I set up the gun mount with a few simple steps. Right leg against the trench wall; left flat on the trench balustrade; MG into the bedding; belt out; load. My gaze traversed the smoke-filled plain feverishly, waiting for targets.

They did not keep me waiting for long. Hundreds of Russians supported by their tanks rose from their trenches like brown waves and forced their way towards us. I felt a shudder down my spine, my heart pounded as if it did not want to accept the spectacle in front of me as reality. With my lips pressed to a thin line, I waited. A well-visible bump in the terrain was set as the firing line. All of a sudden, the MGs of the individual group nests, ours included, rattled off. Shells of our own artillery hissed over our heads and hit close to our positions. This wall of steel and lead left no chance for the Russians to get through. The tanks that had first aimed at us suddenly turned southwest, toward the runway. Apparently, the enemy's main target was not us, but the GJR 144, which was positioned to the right in front of us, by the village of Dniprovska.

After all attacks on us had been averted, we watched the rest of the battle from our slightly elevated positions. Through our cleverly created firing positions, the Russians had received a bloody rebuff. The attackers in their brown uniforms lay in heaps in no man's land. On this day, I came to understand the value of the training I had received in Maribor. Reloading, running, changing position, targeting—everything came naturally now. I was so full of fear during that first battle that it was just my body's automatisms that got me through. The Russians had suffered terrible losses, especially through the flank fire of our MG.

Unlike me, the Alsatian had his nerves well under control. His fire had mowed the Russians down like flies, and eventually they had retreated. Just like that, the big killing had started. And, whether I wanted it or not, there I was, right in the midst of it all.

The enemy was more successful with the 144s, however. As I have mentioned, my school friend Toni served with this unit. He witnessed and survived the battles that day. During one of our chance meetings at the front, he told me more about it. It turned out that, after a long, hard struggle, the enemy finally succeeded in breaking through the lines around the village of Stachanov. The main battle line had soon been broken, and wild carnage had set in. Just as Toni had wanted to push a new loading strip into his sniper rifle, a Russian had jumped on him with a bayonet. Quickly turning aside, he had barely been able to dodge what would have been a fatal blow and, in return, he had smashed his rifle butt into the Russian's head. With all the comrades around him already fallen, he had fought his way back to the company command post, running alongside Russian tanks at times.

There, everyone was struggling for survival. The situation

was so confusing that some Landser (German colloquial term for a German army soldier) even went for each other's throats. The Russian tanks drove over the trenches and headed for the artillery positions. We were able to observe the whole situation from our slightly raised emplacements. Courageous riflemen even tried to place jerrycans on the engine covers of some of the tanks and then tried to set them on fire with targeted shots. A suicide mission that often ended with the death of a brave lone fighter. Eventually, a German counterattack saved the desperate situation, smashing the enemy forces, who had spent the whole morning trying in vain to take the runway to Dniprovska. Left behind were countless dead and a large number of burned-out tanks. This December 19, 1943, marked my baptism of fire. It was one of the most incisive events of my life. Nothing was ever going to be the same. My youthful carefreeness had vanished under the impact of dread and orchestrated mass destruction. Our Oberjäger knew that too. After my evening duty, back in the bunker, he tapped me on my shoulder. In an almost fatherly manner, he handed me a Schnapps from his battered hip flask decorated with an Edelweiss. He said it all in a few short words: "You did well today. You'll get used to it."

Even a novice like me understood why the Russian tanks had tried to take the main supply road. It led through Dniprovska and Vodyane directly to the river crossings of the Dnieper. Dniprovska was basically a poor, muddy steppe village where our advanced supply point and various command posts were based. The center of the universe for us soldiers of 3 GD during those harsh winter months. Our lives depended on its defense. Had we lost Dniprovska, our backward connections would have been cut off. The few makeshift bridges to the north of the river could only be crossed individually. They were not designed for a quick withdrawal, especially not for whole units. This intensity that we had experienced just before Christmas would more or less carry on over the next days and weeks.

The Wehrmachtbericht (Report of the German High Command) of January 1, 1944, reported the following about our combat zone: "The Soviets resumed their attacks at the bridgehead of Nikopol after heavy artillery preparations, supported by tanks and fighter planes. They were pushed back with large counterattacks. The enemy suffered heavy losses. Numerous tanks were destroyed."

These attacks would soon become a daily routine. However, we were confident that we could handle any situation, as long as we had enough ammunition, and the 24th Panzer Division behind us. As for rations, under cover of darkness one or two of our squad had to march to Kamensk and fill everyone's mess tins. On one such trip, I saw many fallen Gebirgsjäger lying on both sides of the road, all wrapped in tarpaulin. They had probably fallen in the battle for Dniprovska. Where the wind had caused the tarpaulin to flutter, I saw horrendous injuries. The bodies were disfigured, some almost beyond recognition. They were missing entire limbs, large holes gaped in chests and stomachs. At least they had a quick death—that's what I secretly thought at the time. During another ration run, a nerve-racking howl erupted and I jumped into the nearest ditch, only just avoiding what I thought to be a "Katyusha" (a Soviet multiple rocket launcher) shelling. But then I quickly realized that it was our own salvo guns, the so-called DO-launchers, that had put the Russian front under fire with their incendiary shells. The missiles whizzed through the air, leaving behind them a thick cloud of smoke that stood out against the night sky. It was a destructive and fascinating spectacle. The shells detonated right on the enemy's main battle line, building a huge wall of fire that shone bright into the night. At this point the earth's crust seemed broken up, like it was about to drag all life into its hot lava core. It was hard to imagine a living soul could still be walking on the opposite side. But the Russian pressure continued. Probably in part thanks to the expanse of their territory, the enemy was able to fall back on near-inexhaustible reserves of manpower.

In the middle of January, some division officers arrived at our little group nest to observe the enemy for a few hours. Shortly thereafter came the order to set up a reconnaissance patrol to check out the Russian positions. The Soviets had apparently brought in new reserves. This was to be done by day and in relatively good visibility; suffice to say we felt uneasy doing this. The terrain was flat so there was little chance of success. Our Oberjäger led us. If we would hesitate, or if the fear stuck in our bones and stopped us from moving, he made gestures encouraging us to catch up.

It did not take long until the Russians realized our intentions. Just after the first shots were fired, our much-valued group leader was fatally hit. Using heavy counterfire we managed to retrieve our fallen comrade and return to base without any further losses. I hardly knew him, but the sudden and needless death of the South Styrian meant a big blow for the entire group. His caring and thoughtful manner had bound us together and turned us into a well-rehearsed combat unit in a short period of time. More importantly, he had taught us how to survive on the Russian front.

The officers probably saw in it a confirmation that something was brewing on the other side and left our group nest shortly after dark. A squad of Landser came and took our fallen Oberjäger back to Kamenka, where he was laid to rest with the others. The ground was so deeply frozen that graves could only be blown into the ground with concentrated loads. And these loads were needed for battle. A young Fahnenjunker (NCO) arrived with the next nightly ration run. He had just started his front probation and immediately took command of our small group of five soldiers. Life had to go on.

By January 1944 the temperatures could fall no further. An icy easterly wind blew even stronger than usual across the lowlands of the Dnieper. This left our group shelter freezing cold. We had a small stove, but fuel was always in short supply. Behind us lay Kamenka, one of the characteristic poor rural Ukrainian villages that are not even marked on any map. Wooden roofs had already been claimed by the flames. One night we rummaged around in the attic of a house looking for some dry wheat for our stove. The Alsatian only briefly shone his flashlight, but it was long enough for the Russians. They immediately opened fire, using a large-caliber machine gun. The projectiles literally hissed around our ears as we hurried out. Luckily, we had found something flammable and were able to heat our bunker that evening.

It sounds paradoxical, but at the front, people quite often put their lives at risk for those banalities that seem so natural in civilian life. On one occasion I wanted to get rid of the lice in the sweater I had brought from home. It was full of them; if I had put it down, it would have crawled across the bunker floor by itself. I had not washed in at least a month. I placed my warmest garment on the then still-lukewarm hotplate. A reckless thing to do, as, shortly afterward, I fell asleep only to wake up to the stench of my burned jumper. There was nothing left of it worth saving, and from now on I would just be that little bit colder. The Alsatian joked that at least I had managed to get rid of the lice.

During the last days of January 1944, the Russians tried once more to break through our lines. They sent huge amounts of material and men into the field. My gunner 1 and I were in combat almost all the time. To enable us to shoot continuously and more accurately, our MG 42 was set on a tripod mount. While my gunner 1 was firing at the Red Army men rushing toward us with a ghastly "Urrrah," I as gunner 2 was mostly responsible for sighting and for supplying new ammunition belts. At that time, ammunition was not yet scarce; otherwise, we would have never been able to hold this patch of soil for such a long time. In the end, the Russians made their breakthrough a little further north of us, making our positions at the bridgehead untenable. Using strong tank forces and hoping to encircle us, the enemy tried to gain as much space as possible as fast as possible. This hope was soon to be fulfilled.

On February 1, a dispatch runner arrived at our group nest together with our ration run and delivered our withdrawal order. We were only to take our kitbags and ammunition. Everything else, all the things we could not carry ourselves, was to be loaded on horse-drawn carts which were waiting further back. That same night, a handful of infantrymen of the adjacent division came marching in to take over our entrenchments. Unlike us, they were relatively badly equipped. We had lined winter anoraks and felt boots, while these infantrymen wore only the long Wehrmacht coats and hob-nailed marching boots. Emaciated as they were, I doubted they would be able to hold the position for long. I showed an almost ancient infantryman where we kept our spare ammunition. He accepted my briefing with resigned indifference and retired into the warm shelter. Whenever we fought together with comrades who also wore the Edelweiss on their caps, I was confident; but when we had to rely on the army's normal infantry divisions—or, even worse, rogue combat groups—disaster was usually on the menu. I often noted huge differences within the Wehrmacht's forces, not to mention the differences between the forces of the Wehrmacht and its allies.

We finally broke away from our positions in the early morning of February 2 and marched back toward Nikopol.

Our target was the highly frequented Dnieper crossing. As if nature had conspired against our retreating army, thaw began to hamper our efforts right from the start. Add sleet to this, and it very quickly turned the trails into bottomless bogs. We made relatively good progress on the eastern side of the Dnieper, but down by the river crossings we met chaos. A huge military worm had snaked its way from the steep Dnieper embankment far into the hinterland. Hundreds of trucks, tracked vehicles, and horse-drawn carts stood tightly packed, one behind the other, all waiting for the retreat to continue. Isolated anti-aircraft guns still stood in their positions, threateningly pointing their pipes into the sky. All efforts were made to get the vehicles moving again. Sometimes it took a whole troop to do so. Many horses had died of exhaustion only to block the way for the next one following up.

We Gebirgsjäger found it easier. We had robust pack animals and were making good headway even in these conditions. A patrol of the field police delegated us north, away from the great pontoon bridge. We gave the retreating columns a wide berth and crossed over the Dnieper using only a narrow jetty unsuitable for vehicles. We took up new positions on the western bank to the northwest of Nikopol and secured the ongoing retreat of our troops. This time, enemy contact did not materialize. Nobody knew exactly where the enemy waited. But the rumbling of some cannons coming from the west did not bode well. How far had the Russians advanced? Where were they? Where were their spearheads? Again and again, enormous explosions rose up over Nikopol itself. Apparently, our pioneer units were blowing up all the essential war machinery to stop it from falling into the hands of the enemy. The blazing fires were visible even from our positions. The night sky above the already battered city had turned a ghostly red—a bad omen.

A lot was left behind at the bridgehead of Nikopol. Comrades, animals, material, and, not to forget, the youthful carefreeness of many a soldier who had arrived there with me only a month and a half ago.

War forces its own archaic laws onto you. Laws from which you cannot escape with all the best intentions in the world. The choices were extremely limited at that time: to be wounded, to be taken prisoner, or to die. These were the only ways to escape the Eastern Front. I was eager to avoid all three of them. At least for as long as I could.

CHAPTER 4
WINTER IN UKRAINE

We were lying on the western bank of the Dnieper, together with parts of the GJR 138, when the Russians, coming from the north, entered the open flank of our army corps. For this reason, a few days later we found ourselves heading west. So I said goodbye to the elderly Russian peasant woman in whose house I had found a bed at night, and once again loaded my tripod mount and the ammunition onto a packhorse.

We struggled through the mud. Our felt boots were literally pulled off our feet with every step we took. If you lost a boot with one step, it would have been your sock with the next. Many a comrade swore loudly, but that did not change the situation. There were tracked vehicles battling their way forward to the left and right of the column. Mud flew around our heads. At first, I still wiped it off my camouflage jacket, but soon I gave up this laborious task. It only took a few kilometers before we were all covered in a thick layer of dirt. Only the weapons were preserved. We had rolled them in tarpaulin to keep them functional at all times.

Again and again, we marched past vehicles stuck in the mud. Some of the most beautiful and brand-new trucks were stuck up to their axles in the sodden ground. Helpless crews beside them tried to free them up again, using shovels and wooden planks. We were constantly asked for help. After a while, a higher-ranking officer ordered our company commander to divide us into groups to assist with freeing his motorcade. Apparently, they had loaded vital equipment in Nikopol, and it was to be taken to the nearest loading station as a matter of urgency. Our commander, a young lieutenant from Graz, answered dryly that we were the rear guard and that the Russians were right behind us. The officer and his entourage joined us without further ado. The whole convoy went up in flames in the blink of an eye. Not so vital after all. It seemed that, in the end, his life and that of his men were more important.

A few kilometers later we finally reached the loading station. A picture of horror awaited us. Our blood froze. On the tracks, a half-overturned, half-burning transport train of the Reichsbahn. Some wagons were marked with the Red Cross. This train, intended for the wounded from Nikopol, had been hit by a Russian strafing attack. The worst-hit section was that of the medical staff. Only a few paramedics had survived to care for the wounded. Some surviving Landser with bandaged heads and torn-off limbs tried to free themselves from the burning wagons. We quickly jumped in to save what could be saved. I pulled a soldier with a thick head bandage from the fire and put him with a group of other wounded men. But just as I wanted to jump up again, he grabbed my arm and pulled me down close to his face. Muttering incomprehensible words, he took his wedding ring from his finger and pressed it into my hands. I was paralyzed by the dramatic gesture and the glare of his glassy eyes.

A sharp call pulled me away from this unreal situation. The Alsatian shouted over to me, "Get the MG tripod ready, the Russians are already in sight!" I quickly put the ring back on the dying man's finger and ran back to my packhorse. This, like many other moments of this war, was to stay with me for the rest of my life.

As I ran, enemy bullets already whistled around my head. And to make matters worse, they had hit our packhorse. I found it in a puddle of mud, stretching and gasping, burying part of the MG ammunition under it. I unbuckled the gun mount, grabbed one of the ammo boxes, and ran back to the Alsatian, who had already taken up position at the railway embankment. Our first bursts of fire were already well-aimed. Some of the Russians who had been approaching in a wide line threw their hands up in the air. This, in turn, gave the rest of our comrades enough of a breather to get into position. Lying in a semicircle, we spent all night in this fateful place. No trucks to carry off the wounded. And if there had been, they would have gotten stuck in the mud. Anyone slightly able to walk or limp made his way westward, some supported by comrades. As if the enemy sensed we were in a hopeless situation, they left us alone that night. Only the flickering of the burning wagons illuminated the skies of the steppe. Here and there, one could hear the sound of isolated shots. Probably a last act of mercy a seriously wounded man had received from a comrade.

There was deadly silence the next morning. No sign of the enemy far or wide. As we had no one behind us, and our first lieutenant had no further orders, we broke away from our positions and started marching west. Once again past the charred carriages. Passing through this dwelling of death one last time. We stuck to the railway tracks, mainly because there were no other landmarks. Every hundred yards or so we encountered more dead Landser, some awkwardly crouched in the mud, others lying on the tracks. At one point, we found a bunch of bandaged comrades nestled together in death. Because I could not stand the sight of these terrible scenes anymore, I fixed my gaze on the back of the man in front me. As much as possible, for over and over I was forced to climb over corpses, which sent shivers down my spine each time. This terrible situation had made one thing very clear: I did not want to end up like that. I had to get through this, one way or another. The very thought of breathing out my life in the Ukrainian mud summoned the last reserves I had left in me.

After what seemed like endless hours of marching, we finally arrived in a small village full of German troops. A rumor that the Russians had already outstripped us quickly made the rounds. A group of German officers stood around a large map, discussing what to do next. In a nutshell, the mood was depressingly low. We occupied squalid houses and fell into a death-like sleep. The next morning we received our first warm meal in a long time. A few Landser of our unit had slaughtered a young horse and turned it into a stew. Even though we had been told in training that you should never go into combat with a full stomach, I filled myself up, knowing that I was likely looking forward to many more days of starvation. If you sustained a shot to a full stomach, your chances of survival would be extremely low. But all that means nothing when you are physically exhausted and almost starving!

We distributed the last of our ammunition and received short orders, and off we were again. Our heavy company was to move further west. We were to take up positions to stop enemy attacks from the flank. So we spent the next few days in a shallow depression filled with water. Completely soaked and shivering with cold. I had packed the MG ammo into my backpack. Firstly, to protect it from the dirt, and secondly, to make it easier to carry.

Sure enough, it did not take long before the Russians attacked. I do not remember the exact day, but it must have been mid-February. There was thick fog. The visibility in the otherwise flat, barren land was reduced to a few feet. Suddenly we heard a shot, closely followed by a loud, throaty scream. By now I was wide awake. My eyes searched the white nothing for clues. Then another shot, followed by machine-gun fire. Suddenly our MG position was surrounded by frenzied battle noise. The Alsatian moved the MG uneasily from one side to the other, as far as the mount would let him. Using my self-loading rifle and leaning close to his back, I secured our rear. There, a passing figure. Ours? Russians? Our MG rattled. Behind us, I saw two collapsed Russians perforated with bullets. Suddenly another figure appeared to the right. My shot immediately sent him to the ground. To our left we heard Russian commands. I turned the tripod mount quickly in the direction of the sound, and the Alsatian chased a whole belt of ammo into the void. Screams. More Russian commands and then, silence. We squatted tightly on the ground. What next? I was expecting a hand grenade at any moment, but nothing happened.

Many hours later, hours that felt like days, the fog lifted and finally unveiled the battlefield. We saw a dozen dead Russians surrounding us in a semicircle. One wore a peaked cap—probably a commissioned officer. But where was our lot? Calls using the parole died away in the sheer vastness, unanswered. So we stayed in our position for the time being. Later that night a flare rose behind us. The Alsatian went to investigate and came back with bad news. Our company had been badly hit during the slaughter in the fog. The lieutenant had fallen, together with many other comrades. Some Jäger (rifleman private of the German mountain troops) had been badly wounded. The remaining men were to gather further back. A sergeant had taken command. Little did I know that this sergeant was to accompany me throughout the war, and that he would turn out to be one of the reasons why I am still alive today. We continued westward under cover of night.

Once again, we were following the railway embankment, hoping to find a connection somewhere. Here and there we came under fire, but we did not fire back in order to save the little ammunition we had left.

The next few days passed by in a haze. The situation had become desperate. Even though our squad had managed to get by without any losses since we had left Nikopol, death now struck that much faster and crueler. First, it caught our squad leader, the Fahnenjunker on front probation. He took a straight hit to the face. A bullet from an enemy sniper. As he fell over, his head sank up to his ears into the mud. There was a gaping hole at the cervical vertebrae base, smoldering with white vapor. Parts of his brain mass lay in his hood, as if someone had deliberately put it there. I surrendered to this awful sight right on the spot. Shortly thereafter, our remaining three riflemen were assigned to a raiding party whose task it was to free a village. The Alsatian and I stayed behind to provide cover fire. Only one of the party returned, lips trembling. The village was taken. The march continued. Then, unexpectedly, a raging blizzard set in. Once again the temperature sunk, and the muddy landscape around us was covered in a smooth sheet of ice. I carried on, lethargic and bone-weary by now. Under the weight of the tripod mount I fell to the ground. Again and again. As my condition grew ever more hopeless, the Alsatian took the tripod and threw it aside. There was no one left to carry it. But even this relief was only brief. My legs kept giving out. Death was close, too close. But my comrade kept pulling me up. A revivifying slap here, a kick up the backside there, using words which would echo in me for a long, long time:

"Hans … come on, keep going, until the eyes shut …"

In the meantime, the blizzard raged on. Again and again, the marching column had to stop. Comrades simply collapsed and remained on the ground. In most cases, those who were no longer able to walk had to be left behind. This meant sure death, especially in these freezing temperatures. Then again, captivity was not an option either. We knew that the Russians took no prisoners. At some point, a column appeared alongside us. Initially, we thought they were our own—but then we heard snippets of Russian words! I quickly aimed my self-loading rifle at one of the shadowy outlines. Pulled the trigger and ... nothing! The gun lock had frozen. The enemy had noticed us too and instantly began to shoot. "Kneel, MG on the shoulder!" shouted my gunner 1. My shoulder became the makeshift gun mount. I pressed myself against the bipod with full force. The MG rattled in short bursts, almost tearing my eardrums apart in the process. Some of the shadows we spotted earlier fell to the ground. The rest retreated into the blizzard. We marched on.

Finally, a number of burned-out farmhouses appeared out of nowhere. They had heaps of straw piled high between them. Attracted by the only shelter this inhospitable landscape had to offer, we rushed in to dig burrows into the straw piles. No commands were required for this mission. Everyone was most eager to escape from this hell of ice. The fact that the Russians were obviously very close was regarded as the lesser evil. There was no question of fighting anyway. With only one meter's visibility and these arctic temperatures, even the enemy had to give in to nature. The Alsatian, the surviving rifleman, and I huddled together in a small burrow. We were the only ones remaining out of the whole MG squad. Only then did I realize that our young comrade had been hit during the collision with the Russian column. His padded anorak was soaked with blood right below his belt. I carefully reached under his jacket and felt a warm, soft mass. To our horror, a bullet had slashed his stomach wide open, causing his bowels to protrude. A sure death sentence. Without fast and professional medical care, there was nothing left to do.

Condemned to helplessness, we put the young Jäger between us and covered him with a sheet of canvas.

He lived through the whole day and finally died the following night. During this time, he kept calling for help. Just before he died, he thought he saw his mother and calmed down a bit. I rested my hand on his shoulder. I did not want him to die alone. He finally left our world with his eyes wide open and his hands pressed over his intestines. A soldier's fate. Without glitter and glory. Part of the program on the Eastern Front. Nevertheless, it left me profoundly shocked.

The following days, I felt a dull emptiness inside. In the meantime, the snowstorm raged on relentlessly. Our sergeant arrived only once in our burrow. He brought cold food which we devoured straight away. On that occasion, we also gave him half of the dog tag of our dead comrade. What might his parents have felt when they received their son's death notice, weeks later? A horrible thought that cannot be put into words.

As soon as the weather picked up, fighting did too. We fended off some attacks against the village and used up the last of our ammunition. It was only the well-located barrage of our own artillery—who had somehow managed to bring a few howitzers from Nikopol—that saved us from complete annihilation. In the end, the enemy lay in heaps before us once again. After our straw pile had been set alight by tracer fire, we received further marching orders. Like so many others before him, our young comrade was left behind somewhere in southern Ukraine. By now the whole company had shrunk to less than thirty men. Surprisingly, during the march, some assault guns appeared alongside us, taking us further west. I sat on the rear engine cover, and for the first time in weeks I felt a cozy warmth. Burned out as our troop obviously was, we were pulled out of the front and brought across the Ingulets on a makeshift bridge. Then we marched north toward a new base of operations. The surviving parts of the

3rd GD were rearranged. Plenty of food and new winter clothing were distributed. We even had replacements assigned to us. I had arrived in Nikopol toward the end of 1943 together with Field Replacement Battalion 11. The replacement battalion that had just arrived had the number 14! In other words, since my arrival less than two months ago, the division had received nearly three thousand men and was still far below battle strength. The result of the terrible bloodletting of uninterrupted combat. Everyone wondered how long this could carry on for. For the time being, however, we felt safe. Especially because of the river, our new frontline, and the relatively well-built positions that we had moved to.

The temporary rest was a godsend. I even got back to my pocket diary to write down some of the most important experiences of the last few weeks and also a few lines to my loved ones. In between sentry duties, the Alsatian and I took it in turns to conduct field training for the new MG operators. It was less than a year ago that I had been in basic training myself. Now I had to pass the main tricks of the trade on to the newcomers. The aim of the training could be summed up in one word: survival! The crucial lessons were quickly explained:

(1) The MG is the most important weapon of the infantry squad and therefore attracts enemy fire. Especially from heavy weapons and snipers. For this reason, the MG must always be dug in as deep as possible. The muzzle must not protrude more than a hand's width above the ground. Everything else must disappear completely into the ground.

(2) A firefight is very rarely led from the primary position. Most of the time this position is already known to the enemy before the attack begins, and he will target it. Therefore, it is crucial that an MG team set up two to three alternate or supplemental positions that can be quickly occupied under cover.

(3) Fire delivered on the flank of a target has the greatest effect. Ideally, from a position out of direct enemy view. That was one of the first things I learned from the Alsatian. When flanking, the enemy has to literally move through a sheaf of fire, and is usually taken down fast. If using the MG from the front, it must be aimed at each soldier individually.

(4) The barrel must be changed after a maximum of 400 shots. Otherwise, the gunner risks auto-ignitions or, even worse, sleeve tears, which are very difficult to fix. In winter, one must not place the glowing barrel in the snow. This will cause it to warp and render it useless.

(5) If available, mount the gun on the tripod. One can shoot much more accurately and further with it than with the bipod. The Russian method of attack with its wave-on-wave storms was particularly murderous. All you really needed to do was push the machine gun from one curb to the other and let the belt rattle through. The rest would then be finished off by long, uniform bursts of fire.

The young riflemen listened attentively. Some asked cautious questions. I hoped they had understood my instructions. At the end of the day, my survival depended on it too.

It did not take long for a new call to sacrifice to reach us. By early March, the Russians had refilled their storm divisions and begun with isolated attacks. Uncoordinated, and without any tank support—at least for now. In addition, the river was too big a barrier. As was often the case, however, the enemy made their first breakthrough further north. Being simple Landser, we did not notice this until our chain of positions was pulled further apart. If we had previously held to the east, we now secured to the north. At first as a company in a long chain, then as a group nest, and in the end, it was only our little MG squad once again, our line of sight reaching only as far as the neighboring hole. On the morning of March 7,

Russian tanks broke through the full width of the neighboring section, and the drama took its course again. I could see the steel monsters headed for every single dugout and turn on their tracks on the spot, crushing the Landser below. Without anti-tank weapons, the situation was hopeless. Gradually, surviving Jäger rose from their holes and hurried backward. Panic reached us like the plague. Just as our left and right neighbors were heading off, the Alsatian said to me, "Come on Hans, we're cut off." Never before had I folded the gun mount so quickly. We were running as fast as we could. Russian tanks on our heels like the devil. Eventually, we arrived at a German artillery position. By then we were utterly exhausted. With their barrels down all the way, their guns targeted the armored vehicles and stopped them for the time being. There were confused Landser running around everywhere, orders were being given, but there was no trace of the bulk of the company.

Finally, the sergeant arrived. He had obviously left the position as the very last man and was completely out of breath. Wide-eyed, he hurriedly looked around, probably looking for his remaining men.

"Sergeant!" a voice sounded sharply from behind. An artillery officer in impeccable uniform approached and started a screaming concert. "You bastard, why did you and your men break away from your positions!? If I have to blow up my guns because of you, your neck is on the line!"

There were, in fact, no trucks or horse-drawn carts available. Just three or four guns in open firing positions. It was not long before the sergeant had gathered his senses. When he opened his mouth, I heard the familiar hard and casual East Styrian dialect.

"You can kiss my ass, sir. If you wait until Ivan rolls over us, then it's your own fault!" At the same time, he opened his camouflage jacket and revealed a proud collection of medals.

"I will forget the 'bastard' bit for now. You do what you've got to do, but I am going to dig myself back in over there with the boys."

He then turned away from the open-mouthed artillery officer and gave a few grumpy instructions to the surrounding Landser. He also gave a quick order to us, and we went back to lying in the dirt.

Episodes like these were almost a daily occurrence. Especially when you bumped into other troops in the heat of battle. The tone amongst us Gebirgsjäger was always very direct. This may be related to the fact that the troops and the NCOs were mostly recruited from the peasantry. It certainly did not mean that the Jäger were lacking discipline or behaved in a rebellious way; on the contrary, we all had to drink from the same cup of death and distress, and we had a tacit understanding that it would be easier to empty that cup together. During the grind of the Eastern Front, the Gebirgsjäger, who had already been hardened by life in the countryside, collapsed much less frequently than, for instance, the more cultured comrades from the big cities. That is probably why the enemy as a whole was superior to us. He was much more familiar with the terrible climate and the spatial conditions than we were. Rough nature is known to shape tough people. And in their harshness with themselves and with others, the Russians were great teachers.

The superordinate events of the time have been well documented. It is now clear that by March 10 the enemy's mechanized units had already cut our divisions off from their backward connections. This was around the time we were at the artillery position. The subsequent defensive battles against Russian attacks from the north are also well documented. In the following days filled with ever-shifting battles, we moved further and further to the west. One day in defense, the next in attack.

I remember an attack on the village of Malejwka. Not because of any scenic features—the village looked just like any other in Ukraine—but because it was there that I set eyes on the Russian cavalry for the first time. Shortly after having taken the village, the Alsatian and I had settled under the approximately waist-high roof of a building on the outskirts. By then ammunition was extremely scarce and we had not had any food for quite some time. From our slightly elevated fire position, we had a good view over the vast plain. In order to create as wide a firing field as possible, I had cut a large piece off the thatch. We took it in turns and waited. This also meant that who wasn't on guard could warm up a bit next to the farmer's oven. The oven was built differently from the ones in my homeland. The hearth was low, almost on the ground. Above it stood a broad, rectangular base made from clay that was mostly covered with straw and had a horizontal ledge with a cooking plate on top. So kitchen and sleeping spot in the same place. Once warm, the clay retained the heat for a long time. You could still sleep comfortably on the straw bed even if the room had cooled down. The fact that this way you got filled with bugs that sucked even more life from your already drained body, is a different story.

In order to be able to raise the alarm quickly, I had strung a cord down to a bucket with a stone attached to the end of it. Just as I was lying there, listening to the Alsatian's loud snoring and thinking about all the delicacies my homeland had to offer, I saw them coming: Russian cavalry at full gallop. Wide apart but in large numbers. The village was completely quiet. Had no one else noticed anything? Could I really see that much further from my raised position? I began to shake the string and heard the tinny clonk of the bucket. Nothing! I crept toward the attic hatch and lowered my head into the room. "Alarm! The Russians are here!" To my astonishment there was no movement, not even a stir. The Alsatian was out cold, probably due to the exertions of the last few days. Ah, well. I quickly crawled back to my MG. But where was the enemy? There, in the distance, a chain of riders, but where was the rest? Seconds seemed like endless minutes as I fiercely scanned the terrain, the MG at the ready.

All of a sudden, a wave of horsemen jumped out of a hidden depression, sabers drawn. Not even 200 meters away. They were so easy to target I only needed my front sight. I pulled the trigger, sending my salvos out to meet them with a loud, short staccato. *Brrrr, brrrr, brrrr.* The first horses suddenly fell. Jumping wildly, hurling their riders from their saddles. There was only occasional gunfire to the left and right of me, until the whole thing crescendoed into hellish battle din. Suddenly the Russian cavalrymen flowed left and right past my range of fire and straight into the village. It was a bit like Moses parting the sea. The next wave followed quickly out of the depression and I continued firing. In all the excitement I did not even notice the Alsatian lying down next to me. Not until he handed me the next strap. This too was soon used up. Then, a barrel change and the last strap. As this one grew ever shorter, I got more careful with where I placed my sheaves. By now, the Russian infantry had come closer, their bullets hissing through the thatched roof. We were forced to get out of the attic. We headed downstairs, leaving the MG behind. We defended our position through the windows left and right of the farmhouse with our semi-automatic carbines. Almost every shot was a hit. Enemy cavalrymen rode that close up that I could have literally grabbed hold of them. I was expecting a hand grenade at any moment now. That would have been the end of us. Wounded comrades came and dropped into the corner. Since I was running out of ammunition, I crawled over to one of them and took some clips to reload. He, a young lad, had a severely bleeding wound on his neck and was begging for help, but I had no choice. I had to return to the window and keep fighting. The battle lasted for quite a while and finally ebbed away. There were riderless horses galloping about, other horses stood lethargically for a short while and then collapsed, their bodies littered with bullets. Wounded soldiers, friend and foe, crawled through the mud between the houses. A nightmarish scene in which humanity faded away like the faces of the dead soldiers in the Russian winter.

I was glad to see the Alsatian in front of me. He slipped the MG belt from a wounded man's neck, gave me a short nod, and climbed back up into the attic. Seconds later I heard the MG click-clacking and knew that he would watch over us. The battle noise subsided and was followed by the desperate cries for paramedics. I turned to the comrade screaming the loudest and began to tie off his foot. The wide pool of blood below his knee and the shredded trousers indicated to me that an artery may have been hit. When the army doctor finally arrived with a couple of his assistants, his instructions echoed like gunshots:

"Bandage, morphine—pressure bandage—nothing left to do with this one—dead—head bandage …"

My eyes fell on the young comrade with the neck wound, the one I had taken the ammunition from. He sat hunched over as if he were asleep. His two bloodied hands were still pressed against the wound. His broken look was fixed on the dirty clay floor as if he were staring into the distance. Too late. Why had I not helped him? This damned war!

As pointless as it was, we had to continue, even if it was just to get us and the wounded out of there.

The heavy sacrifice in the fight against the Russian cavalrymen had marked a new low. The troop was completely burned out. Ammunition was in short supply, not to mention food. This time the enemy had appeared from all sides. We all knew what that meant. We had no choice. The division had to risk everything and make for the Bug. The river was the only reasonably close anchor point that promised something akin to safety. At least in the theories of the military strategists. In the days after this attack, everything seemed to point toward this breakout. First, we dragged ourselves further west and once again started scraping positions into the frozen ground somewhere in the icy steppe. There, we defended ourselves against some undecisive attacks. Then we were gradually drawn to a larger village. All sorts of arms and divisional units had already accumulated there. The houses were filled to the brim with wounded soldiers. Even some assault guns rolled slowly across the muddy village streets, groups of filthy Gebirgsjäger perched on top. I had just made myself useful lashing some boxes onto a packhorse when I heard a familiar voice:

"Hans, have they promoted you to stable boy now because you are of no use at the front?"

It was Toni, my school friend, waving at me with a beaming smile. He jumped off the back of an assault gun together with another Landser and we fell into each other's arms. Toni was with the 144s, our sister regiment, and apparently everyone was gathering here for the upcoming breakout. Our meeting was such a joyous event that the drama around us seemed to stand still. We quickly exchanged our different experiences of the past few weeks. Toni had much better insight into the overall situation. Being a sniper, he often took his orders directly from the company and battalion command posts. Snipers always worked in pairs, and he introduced me to his comrade. That morning they had still been the rearguard against the enemy, stopping the oncoming Russians with targeted shots. Since I had last seen him, he had even been awarded the Iron Cross 2nd class for a particularly risky mission at the Ingulets.

The joyful reunion lasted only for a short time. We all had to carry on. Orders were shouted and we said our goodbyes. Just before he left, he fumbled half a loaf of bread out of his backpack and gave it to me.

"Here, take this. They say it's about 10 kilometers and then we should be through."

I watched the pair disappear in a group of our comrades.

That hunk of bread was a godsend. Though it was rock-hard, it went down like a Wiener schnitzel. The Alsatian and I devoured it with greedy bites. For the rest of the day, we went back to help with the packhorses and unload wagons. Anything that was expendable was thrown away or burned. This was to make room for the wounded. Trucks and half-track vehicles started arriving. The latter almost overflowed with soldiers and still had guns attached to the back. The redeeming order came just after dusk, and it called for a last show of strength. As a hurriedly thrown-together combat group we had to take a railway line held by the enemy. We were to advance southwest as quickly as possible. Somewhere on the way, there would be a meeting point. Everything was improvised, but the prospect of an end to the nightmare was motivation enough to carry on.

So our column set off once again in one long line. Man behind man, face to back. There was no sound but comrades wheezing and weapons clinking. The night was pitch-black. How far was that railway line? What was out there waiting for us? I was constantly expecting our column to change into a skirmish line, or a surprise fire attack. The column stopped from time to time, but then carried on again. Then, after many hours, sudden loud clapping followed by cautious cursing. And then again. And again. Until I myself finally stumbled over an obstacle on the ground. And lo and behold, there it was: the railway track! But where had the Russians slept that night? It was beyond me. Had they also been at the end of their strength, and just wanted to have a rest? We reached the small river early in the morning and without any incidents. Using planks and boards, the awaiting pioneers had created a relatively wide crossing. It was flooded in places, but it held.

As we moved further west, we were joined by ever more columns. Infantry parts, artillery, but also numerous retinue units consisting of a hodgepodge of wagons. When the march finally came to a halt, we were served our first warm meal in two weeks. The breakout had been achieved, even though it had not felt like it. But just for once, why should we not be the lucky ones? Everyone was relieved. Though there were no visible signs of it. Especially not with the young comrades. Too emaciated, too exhausted. What we had been through in the last few weeks had exceeded every soldier's imagination. It was no longer justifiable as a mere fulfillment of duty or service to the fatherland. The constant fear of death, the hunger, the unbelievable physical exertions, all without any rest—not to mention the mass destruction and killing of humans and animals alike. All this had eaten a deep hole into our souls. It was just like our elders said. It had turned us into a new breed: the Eastern Front fighter!

CHAPTER 5

RACE FROM THE BUG TO THE DNIESTER

Once we arrived in our new combat zone near Novo-Belousova, all companies were reorganized. It was high time too, given the enduring chaos. On March 19, 1944, my pocket diary shows the following note: "Collecting the 4th (heavy) Company. 23 men." We had been below our nominal strength of 140 men since Nikopol, even with further comrades joining us along the way. The bloodletting had been indescribable. Of course, for one fallen soldier there were always two or three wounded ones. However, getting them out was not as easy as during the recent breakout.

The well-developed positions at the Bug were remnants from our advance in 1941. We were able to overlook the wide river quite well. The enemy was on the high ground opposite, outside the reach of any infantry weapons. Initially, this restricted fighting to sporadic mortar and artillery shelling. Buried deep in the ground, we finally enjoyed some peace, at least for now. The command was led by the highly decorated East Styrian sergeant, the very man who had joined us at the bridgehead of Nikopol at the beginning of the retreat. That gave us courage. He always knew exactly what to do. Little was known about him, for he kept a certain distance from us subordinates, but we knew he cared. Down in the trenches, it was often rumored that he had been a simple woodcutter before the war. Others thought he had made his living as a wandering blacksmith. Nobody knew for sure. Almost thirty years old, he had been involved in the engagements since the Polish campaign. Four and a half years of war! It was also certain that he had a wife and children. In the safety of the bunker I often found him staring at a picture the size of a postcard. He held it almost devoutly in his rough, furrowed hands, looking at it for several minutes at a time. In the flickering of the Hindenburg light I could make out the contours of a slender woman with three small children. They seemed to be laughing. On one occasion, he must have felt my eyes on his back. He quickly slipped the picture back under his camouflage jacket and then turned away from me, snarling. I was mortified. I had not intended for my youthful curiosity to destroy this intimate moment for him. That night I thought about the scene for a long time—about the deep longing for his loved ones that must have burned in his heart. What else did fate have in store for him?

All sorts of replacements arrived with the marching battalion 3 GD/15. Soldiers returning from vacation and some that had recovered from their wounds. Not just new faces, but familiar ones too. Many a lost comrade had returned and brought us hours of joy.

After a few quiet days it was time for the Alsatian to go home on leave. His leave was long overdue, after one and a half years at the front. Because he had always talked about it, I asked him to bring back some beef jerky from his region. I was hoping for a reunion with this impeccable man. Be it at the front or in the aftermath of the war.

The sergeant immediately promoted me to gunner 1,

calling me an "experienced Landser." A young farmer's son from Gleisdorf near Graz was placed by my side. From now on I had to set the tone. I was barely nineteen years old.

One morning they announced the arrival of the mail. Down in the bunkers this clearly caused a sensation. Soon two mounted soldiers arrived with all sorts of bags loaded onto their cart. The men looked almost reverently at the two comrades as they took it in turns reading out the names on the parcels and letters.

"Brandner – Here! – Steinlechner – Here! – Riegler – Here! ..."

As the company postal bags emptied more and more my heart started pounding. "Lang – Here! – Posch – Here! ..." Would I be left empty-handed? The tension was unbearable. Receiving mail at the front was like Christmas and Easter falling on the same day. For people in peacetime this might be unimaginable, but for us, apart from going home on leave, it was the best surprise. Close to the end, I finally heard the redeeming "Kahr."

"Here! Here I am!" My voice almost broke with excitement. I quickly grabbed the package and retired to the bunker. It had a Fürstenfeld postmark, so it had to be from my father. And indeed it was. The package yielded all sorts of treasures I had been dreaming about for months. Bacon, smoked sausage, a jar of honey, and much, much more. Most of it came from our farm and some of it from the butcher in the village. Sitting on top of it all was a long letter from my father. I read it over and over. He wrote about the wood stores for winter, the health of the cattle, and the family, of course. About how worried he was about me. Not only because he had fought on the Eastern Front himself, but also because of the many casualties the village had mourned by now. He also mentioned a package he had sent in January, but it had never arrived. It must have made it to the front during our chaotic retreat. Or it had fallen into the hands of the Russians. This would also happen from time to time. Anyway, my longing for a good peasant snack and news of my relatives was satisfied for now. And for just a moment, the war seemed almost forgotten.

Any historian will know that silence is deceptive. While the division, the corps, and indeed the whole army were being patched up, the enemy also took the opportunity to draw new strength from his gigantic empire. Strengthened by the Allies' relief deliveries, which increased month by month. The Russians had replenished their rifle, cavalry, and mechanized divisions in no time, including many of their dreaded guard units. Fully motorized or on horseback, these were equipped with artillery, ammunition, and tank resources, which the German troops had been lacking for a long time. We had had a lucky escape at Nikopol and also at the Ingulets. And even though we had taken a huge hit, our front line to the east was closed once again. It was, however, almost certain that the enemy would not repeat the mistakes they had made, especially the dispersal of their spearheads during our last escape.

A new, all-embracing battle was about to emerge on the horizon. The cruel struggle was due to begin once more.

On March 26, under the cover of darkness, the Russians sailed across the Bug on inflatable boats and wooden ferries. Flares were already rising as the Gleisdorfer comrade and I stormed out of the bunker. There were a few scattered shots, but no trace of the enemy. In the distance, the dull sound of fire. Seconds later, the first hits of artillery shells. They landed right behind us. *Pfffff.* Another flare marked the night sky and floated slowly to the ground. The flickering, yellowish light gave me a chance to take note of the shadowy lowlands of the Bug. The flat slope was followed by a reed belt. Behind it, the smooth, pitch-black river.

Pffff. The next flare shot up into the sky. Slowly, my eyes got used to the darkness. Over there: movement on the river. This was quite unimpressive at first, but then I could make out the outlines quite clearly. With the MG taut between my chin and shoulder, I picked out a possible target and pulled the trigger. The tracer bullets rushed toward the water like lightning, only to vanish inconclusively into the dark. Another sheaf. A third. Suddenly, one of the tracer bullets bounced off of something and pulled sharply to the side. No doubt here, the enemy was coming across the water! So I fired belt after belt, waiting for a ricochet every time. Meanwhile, the enemies' artillery hits were so close I had to pull the MG back into the ditch. The dirt flew up around us. The second the last lumps had hit the ground, the MG came up again, above the parapet, and we continued firing.

"Three hundred fired—barrel change!" I shouted over to the Gleisdorfer while still taking aim. But nothing happened. I glanced sideways. The Gleisdorfer was crouching on the ground, hands pressed to both ears.

"You damn fool," I yelled, and I gave him a powerful kick. "Move your ass!" I had no time for sensitivities now. Whether or not this was his baptism of fire. This was about more than our own lives.

With the battle inferno increasing, we could finally hear hand grenade explosions and MP salvos coming from the left-facing positions. When in battle, one loses all sense of time. My next clear thought did not appear until the pale morning dawned. Some inflatable boats were still trying to get across the Bug. But they were stopped by either myself or a neighboring MG just as they were trying to board. The Red Army soldiers tumbled off the boats or were hit as they tried to retreat, wading waist-deep through the water. Their bodies floated downstream, dead, leaving a thin, dark-red trail behind them. A gruesome spectacle, with a bitter aftertaste for the one who did it. Now deprived of the protection of the night, the Russians finally gave up. The riflemen dived back into the reed belt. They were immediately swallowed up, as if the ground had opened. Only a few dinghies and wooden ferries remained, scattered along the riverbank. The fighting in the ditches and the lowlands on our side of the Bug continued. It lasted almost the whole morning. The creation of an enemy bridgehead had to be prevented at all costs. If need be in close combat, spade in hand. Fortunately, as part of the heavy company, we'd have nothing to do with that. It was the job of the Jäger platoons to make the final decision. And so we successfully rebuffed another attack.

That evening, while receiving ammunition, I encountered my first Russian prisoners of war. Their heads were shaven, their facial expressions more than grim. Some had such crude Asian features that it seemed they had sprung directly from a Genghis Khan fable. They were sitting on the ground next to the company headquarters. Without any emotion. No fear, no dejection, nothing. "My God," I thought, "how is this going to end?"

The next day it became apparent that the whole front had come back to life. Our section was under heavy artillery fire. Soviet bombers flew northwest. It seemed they didn't notice us at all. I had already suspected that something was brewing. That night, the enemy kept us busy by trying to cross the river once again. But the attempt failed just like the first one. The division had obviously expected another attack. Our own artillery fired a particularly effective barrage. As dawn broke the next morning, we saw whole piles of fallen Red Army soldiers on the opposite side, with all kinds of destroyed amphibious landing and bridging equipment scattered between them. But while the rumble continued further north, things remained perfectly still on our side. There was an increasing nervousness that had made its way into the trenches. And it would not be left at that. The sergeant came in person to deliver the bad news. The look on his face spoke volumes. The day before, the Russians had already completely smashed our neighbors to the north, and their guard units had taken over the Bug further up. But instead of rolling on along the river, his mechanized forces had been pouring into the hinterland. The defense line at the Bug had become untenable. The army had ordered the immediate withdrawal to the Dniester.

"Dniester!? The border with Romania?" I thought. Even by a conservative estimate, it was about 200 kilometers away. Had it not been for the sergeant bellowing his instructions, I would have screamed in desperation.

"Get ready to march! Take as much ammunition as you can carry. Everything else stays behind."

My powerlessness was drowned in the military din and the feverish rush to get out of there in one piece. It took the Gleisdorfer just a few seconds to fold the bipod and shoulder the MG. I in the meantime stuffed my backpack with machine-gun belts. With the semi-automatic and reserve barrel slung across our backs, we trudged toward the company headquarters. It hurt to leave our carefully constructed positions. Blankets, tarpaulins, the stove, everything was left behind.

It was late when we finally marched out into the endless steppe once again, passing some empty mortar positions and abandoned cottages on the way. With the ground frozen underneath us, we made good headway. And due to the heavy load we could hardly feel the cold. The upcoming dawn revealed almost the same picture as twelve hours earlier. It seemed as if we had been marching on the spot, so monotonous and empty was the landscape. Icy rivulets and canyons carved out by erosion were the only clues of any progress. There were no signs of any other parts of the division either. Our little gang of maybe forty men looked like a doomed punitive expedition. The sergeant led the march. Only using compass bearings, at least as far as I can remember. As the day wore on, morale declined at a steady pace. The calls of "How much further?" grew louder and louder. A statement that every soldier, of any nation, knows only too well. Occasionally, the march began to falter, whereupon the sergeant repeatedly ran to the back and drove us Jäger to hurry up. In order to distance ourselves from the imposing Russians, the division had orders to march as far west as possible, as quickly as possible. Stops were only to be made once a day, at predefined defensive lines. Until the Dniester was reached. But where were these defense lines? And above all, what security would they offer?

At a certain point, we were completely exhausted. It was already pitch-dark. We were sheltering in a shallow hollow to protect ourselves from the icy easterly wind. Wherever we stopped, we would just let ourselves fall to the ground and fall asleep immediately. I did the same here. As if I knew something bad was about to happen, I suddenly shot up. I was trembling to the bone. I heard some desperately muffled words in my immediate vicinity and crawled toward them. With my eyes still adjusting to the darkness, I saw the outline of some comrades squatting on the ground.

"Damn. Those bastards!" said the desponding voice of an Oberjäger.

I huddled between two bodies and followed the dimmed beam of a flashlight wandering across the icy ground. It showed a pair of mountain boots, followed by lower legs, then the hips. My blood froze at what was revealed next. Before me lay a torn-up heap of human flesh, pressed tightly into the ground. The upper body and head were a mass of mashed meat and outlines of tissue. Mixed in were some scraps of clothing that might once have been a winter camo. There was a wide chain track leading away from the corpse. Stooping right down, we crept a few meters further until we discovered the next dead Landser. Then another. As horribly disfigured as the first. There was no doubt about it: we were in the middle of a graveyard. Created by Russian tanks that had caught those who had probably left the Bug some hours prior to us. Had they surprised a Gebirgsjäger unit at rest? Or had the comrades fought their last battle here? Was this our first line of defense? Questions the monster called war will never answer. For the relatives of the dead, there would only be a miserable "Missing in the south of the Ukraine," although in the end this message was a thousand times easier to endure than the horrific truth.

After this terrible discovery, it took mere seconds for our will to survive to kick back in. We had to get away from this dwelling of death. The company was on its feet again in no time. The newly awakened joined the long line of dazed marchers. Once again, we delved into the night.

I can only vaguely remember the martyrdom of the next few days. What I do remember, I remember by capturing individual experiences and memories. In a sense, this retreat was a race against the enemy. The state we were in, and with the most adverse weather conditions, we only managed to walk around 3 kilometers an hour. This made it easy for the motorized Russians to outstrip us.

We marched 20 to 30 kilometers a night. At times to the west, then to the south, and in the early hours of each morning we dug ourselves in. Come noon, the Russians had already caught up again. In the evenings, we would break away from our positions and carry on. This went on for days. Sometimes we came across some of our own units, other times we lay alone in the icy steppe, a pocket of resistance.

In order to be able to grasp the terrible suffering and

deprivations of those days, even if it is only to a limited extent, one has to visualize the situation. This was more stumbling than marching, in a trance. Small hordes of Jäger struggling through the endless sparseness of this vast country. We fell asleep at every stop. I usually dropped into the snow on the spot, only to wake up a few minutes later from the freezing cold. Those who went on with a shred of strength left drove their exhausted comrades on. Orders were replaced with kicks and pistol butts. I sucked snow against the terrible hunger. This, in turn, gave me severe stomach cramps. After all, we had long been moving far beyond any humanitarian norm. The instinct of self-preservation—the lowest instinct of mankind—had become the supreme law. If one would let oneself be worn down by hunger, fatigue, cold, and the threat of ever-present death, if one gave up inside, then one was lost forever. It seemed like I was trapped in a never-ending nightmare. My life before the war had completely faded from my memories.

I stared at the back of the man in front of me, the young Gleisdorfer. He had fought bravely so far, but his strength had long since worn away. Again and again, he fell out of line, until he finally fell over to the side. He could barely hold his weapon. And, again and again, I had pulled him up, until one time he just lay there, quietly sobbing. I could barely carry on myself. I had been carrying the MG, the rucksack with the ammunition, and my semi-automatic for quite some time now. I knelt beside him helplessly. The sergeant came forward. With a quick flick of his hand, he gestured for me to leave the machine gun and ammunition behind.

"We are not leaving the boy," was his almost paternal command. "It's not that far anymore," he added, before he went back up front. Seizing the strength of sheer desperation, I clawed my way into the Gleisdorfer's camouflage jacket and gave him a brutal slap in the face.

"Do you want to snuff it here, in the dirt? Damn sure you don't! So come on, lad. Until the eyes shut!"

Back in reality, he shook himself awake and stood up. I dragged him alongside me, neatly tucked under my right shoulder.

The most disastrous psychological effect of the retreat was loneliness. Then there was no bread, no ammunition. Not to mention the missing medical care and support weapons. Agreements with other combat groups about what to do next were made by estimated guesses. How lucky were those Landers, who still had a packhorse. At least they could let it carry the heaviest loads. Everything else rested on the shoulders of the steadily weakening Jäger. Given the miserable situation, it was only too understandable that some soldiers lost their nerve and left their positions at first enemy contact in a panic.

It was sometime in early March. The exact date remains a mystery, as by then I had lost all sense of time and space. That morning, the sergeant had led us to the new resistance line and was assigning positions to individual men. After leaving the MG, I was now degraded to a simple rifleman. Using my hands, I dug a roughly hip-deep hole into the snow and crouched down. As usual, the task was to stop the Russians during the day in order to be able to retreat again during the night. Because of the combat-related casualties of the recent days, our bunch had shrunk even further. This had an impact on our defense line, which was accordingly thin. My closest comrades, who were also alone in their holes, were about 80 meters away.

I suddenly heard the muffled hum of tank engines. The noise made me cringe as if I had been electrified. It was self-evident that this were not our own tanks. I had not seen any of them since the Ingulets. It did not take long until I saw the first T-34 emerge from a slight depression. It was soon joined by others. They quickly made it up to a dozen or so. As I looked left and right, I saw my two comrades craning their necks. They too had realized what was brewing on the other side. Behind us, as always, flat, barren terrain. I realized that this time I might have reached my last hour. I crept deeper into my hole. There was nothing left to do here, especially not with just a handful of exhausted and emaciated Gebirgsjäger. Even an escape to the rear would have been utterly pointless. In this open terrain, these tanks would have crushed us just like they had the comrades we had found in the hollow. I watched the fast-moving war machines in shock. Damned to inaction, looking death in the eye.

Suddenly, a lifesaving sharp bang interrupted the unreal scenery and blew the turret of the foremost T-34 to bits. Unbeknown to all of us, a single German assault gun had taken up a position a few hundred meters behind us. It was now shooting at the Russian tanks at maximum capacity. Three or four T-34 had already burst into flames before the Russians could even locate the assault gun. Another began to spin on its tracks until a fist-like blast to its flank blew the whole thing into several large pieces. Probably assuming this was coming from a somewhat stronger enemy force, the Russians retreated into the shallow while still firing across the terrain. Relief washed over me as I stared at the burning tanks. I silently thanked the assault gun crew who had put their necks on the line for us and who had been victorious.

We all rose from our holes and marched back toward the assault gun. Our "job" for this day was done. Once there, we looked into the faces of the happy crew. They had just lit their cigarettes, visibly relieved about their success in a highly unequal showdown. The assault gun commander was surprised to find German troops here at all. His mission had been to push into no man's land to get enemy contact. It must have been fate for him to appear exactly where a handful of

Landser were facing death. We had been so damned lucky. I still remember that a bag of rusks was dished out, which we immediately devoured right down to the last crumb.

The assault gun also had radio contact with the rear. Our sergeant learned about the next resistance line. After a brief discussion, the weakest of our bunch finally sat on the rear of the tank and moved slowly southwest. It was time to put some more distance between ourselves and the Russians. Many kilometers later we arrived at a small farming village. Here we merged with other combat groups.

Around April 4 or 5 and after another 50 kilometers of marching the die had finally been cast. The 3rd Gebirgsjäger Division, along with the 258th, 294th, 17th, and 302nd Infantry Divisions, had been surrounded close to the city of Rozdilna. The Dniester was within reach. In this hour of extreme need, if one wanted to save the ten thousand or so Landser from certain death, quick and forceful action was needed. The circle itself was only a few kilometers wide and was as flat as a football field. There was no hope for rescue from the outside. The divisions west of us were just as burned out as we were. To top it all off, there was a heavy onset of winter weather, with lots of snow and icy temperatures. Severe frostbite began to spread. In the villages around us, the wounded piled up once again. This time it was only the seriously injured that were kept in semi-sheltered accommodation. The rest of the Jäger, grenadiers, and gunners remained out in the open.

There was only little food left. Was this to be our last ration? The situation seemed completely hopeless. Were we about to suffer the same fate as the hundreds of thousands of German soldiers who had remained in Stalingrad?

Radio messages informed the divisional commander that parts of the 97th Jäger and the 257th Infantry Divisions had formed a kind of safe zone around the Kuchurgan. This had to be reached under all circumstances. According to Divisional Chronicles of the 3rd Gebirgsjäger Division, Regiments 138 and 144 had a combined strength of two weak battalions at the time. The artillery fielded less than a dozen guns. There was only one infantry platoon of pioneers left. Whole units had dissolved into thin air during the course of the retreat.

The Gleisdorfer was lying next to me in the snow, his tired eyes peering across the icy steppe, his face buried deep inside his mountain cap. The metallic Edelweiss on his cap was dirty and bent out of shape.

"Well Hans, they've got us now. We are trapped!" I took my hood off and rummaged in my reversible jacket for a last piece of biscuit to share with my comrade. "Here, have this."

We silently munched on our death row meal. At that very moment a sidecar motorcycle came from behind. An officer got out and rushed over.

"Men. At the ready. We are breaking out. Meeting point is 500 meters south of here. See you in half an hour!"

"Lieutenant, will there be any food?" the young Gleisdorfer asked.

"In Romania, boy, in Romania!"

How right he was.

With our heavily tested division leading the assault, the breakout battle began during the night of April 6, 1944. Without any fire preparation and under the cover of darkness. Once the signal came, we silently rose from our staging area and assembled. Clouds hung in the sky; the moon only sporadically threw its light over the white Ukrainian steppe. A few hundred meters further we hit a Russian ditch, where a Gebirgsjäger took us over. He said that they had already managed to cut down the Russians without a shot being fired.

Without looking back, we carried on toward a little village. The homesteads emerging against the night sky grew bigger and bigger. At the same time, the tension increased. I could hear a Russian post calling for the parole. Then a dull thump. Done. Quick, over to the houses. I pulled a grenade out of my belt and threw it through a window, waiting for the detonation as I pressed myself to the ground. The windows flew off their hinges with a deafening bang. Battle commenced. The raging inferno turned into uncoordinated individual actions. A Russian grabbed me by the neck in one of the peasant huts. We both tumbled to the ground. He hit my head powerfully against something hard. While slowly losing my senses, I used my feet to push him away from me. He stared at me in fury, his Mongol eyes flickering in the light of the burning buildings. In this murderous struggle for survival I fumbled for my knife, and then, in all my fear and panic, I pushed it incessantly between his ribs. His grip weakened after each stab. He finally fell to the side and breathed his last. I jumped onto my dizzy feet and peered out the window. A group of Jäger jumped across the village street only to collapse under machine-gun fire. Some Landser stormed into the peasant hut and tried to push forward through the garden. It was those I joined.

What is dismissed in wartime literature as a "hard struggle" is in reality a slaughter of friend and foe, often characterized by appalling brutality. There is nothing heroic about it. The battle raged on for hours. It went back and forth. Almost all the houses were on fire. The air was filled with lead. Hand grenades were given out in one of the ditches, and a raiding patrol assembled. Ten to twelve men. Machine-gun fire hissed over our heads continuously. Our patrol leader raised his fist to signal the attack. This fist was immediately blown off, leaving only a stump where seconds before there had been a hand. Nevertheless, I hauled myself over the edge of the ditch and broke into the Russian MG position with the others. We killed the machine-gun crew in a frenzy. The enemy immediately began the counterattack, and we had to retreat to our starting position. Half of the men were missing. But our patrol leader forced us up once more. This time his face was pale with the loss of blood from his severe injury. We stormed out of the ditch and hurled our hand grenades at the enemy. Passing some dead Russians and running past the edge of the village, we reached a deep furrow just in time to fend off a second counterattack.

Squinting at the steppe, I saw flares rising into the night. The Russians were on full alert. Just like on the way to the Ingulets, mounted Cossacks stormed in. At first only in small groups. Then in whole packs. What a terrible mess. Everyone was defending their own skin as best as they could. As the fighting lessened, I expected we'd be breaking out soon. Instead, we got the order to hold the position and not to give up an inch of ground. So I spent the next twenty-four hours lying among fallen comrades, dead Russians, and dead horses. Getting any rest was out of the question. Never mind the complete exhaustion. What were we waiting for? Why were we not just getting out of this damn cauldron? This would only make the battle harder. I did not know that the senior leadership had deliberately stopped the breakout for another day. For one thing, they did not know where the neighboring army corps was positioned and needed more time to find out. Secondly, by taking the Russian village, we had blocked the advance of the Russian IV Guards Cavalry Corps. They, in turn, cut off from supplies and threatened with encirclement, withheld any further attacks.

Taking advantage of this situation and using the last of our strength, we finally blew the lid off the cauldron on the evening of April 7. The principal driving force was the fear of falling into the hands of the Russians. Over the next twenty-four hours, thousands of Landser poured down this narrow corridor, which was held against only minor enemy attacks. Once the wounded were through, we also left our positions, dirty and exhausted. The infantry unit entrenched on the other side of the Kuchurgan looked at us as if we came from another planet.

After weeks of the hardest deprivations, where death had found ample booty all around us, I relaxed a bit. I had barely had time to get used to the front line when heavy defensive battles had started by the bridgehead. The fighting parts of the 3rd Gebirgsjäger Division had shrunk to less than a thousand men. An appalling bloodletting, which was characteristic of the overall situation on the Eastern Front. I did not see the young Gleisdorfer again. His trail was lost in the carnage at the village. Those who might have had something to say about his fate had not gotten through either. When I think about him, I still hear the sergeant's words: "We will not leave the boy behind!" And each time an infinite sadness bubbles up inside me.

After our successful breakout, nobody knew how things would continue. Paroles buzzed all around. Once it was said that we would soon be reintegrated into the main battle line. Another time we heard something about being sent home to recharge to full combat strength. But both theories were to be proven wrong. Our next lot was to replenish the division embedded in the Romanian line. Our route was to continue via Tiraspol, heading west toward the Dniester crossing at Tighina, which we reached on April 14. The leftovers of 3 GD now rallied west of the Dniester. Behind us, the flat, rough, snow-laden landscape of Ukraine, holding thousands of fallen and missing comrades.

Once in Romania, the Russian momentum subsided. In the past two and a half months the Red Army had managed to advance about 350 kilometers to the west, causing heavy losses to Army Group South. The enemy had finally turned the tables. There was nothing left of the Wehrmacht's breathtaking 1941–42 successes. The German war machine had increasingly faltered in the never-ending expanses of the Soviet Empire. Add to this the catastrophic terrain and weather conditions, the aid deliveries of the Allies, and the unperturbable fighting spirit of the simple Red Army soldier. Millions of dead and wounded soldiers or even prisoners had failed to have an impact on the Russians. After the victorious "cauldron battle" of Stalingrad, the gentlemen in the Kremlin had found their recipe against Hitler. Lightning-fast attacks using tanks, artillery, and masses of infantry. The German generals got a taste of their own tactics, and they weren't able to turn the tables back around. A statement by the Soviet tank general Rokossovsky sums it up perfectly: "The German army is a machine, and machines can be broken."

Broken—that, we definitely were. After having survived the heavy fighting, the mood of the troops wavered between quiet joy and a sense of foreboding. At the time, did I still believe the war could be won? So I could return to my faithful family at the end of it all? Well, at least I hoped so! Even if hope often reveals itself as a perfidious liar, especially during wartime. At the end of the day, however, it is deeply human to hope. Hope blurs out your own helplessness and is often the only thing you can cling to in many a dark hour.

Anyway. There was no time for philosophizing. There were many physical needs that were much more important. In order to freshen up, we had taken up quarters in a house behind the Dniester. This was the first time in a very long while that I had a roof over my head. Since the beginning of February, to be precise. Finally, time for a proper wash! I used a good deal of soap to scrub the mud, dirt, and physical exudates of the past four months off my skin. That is how the miserable state of my body revealed itself to me. My fat reserves had disappeared due to the constant lack of food. My skin stretched taut over hollow ribs. My stomach was dented, almost as if I was holding it in with all my might. Hands and legs, formerly tight and strong from all the agricultural work, had degenerated into dry branches.

But that was not all. Beneath the layer of dirt I found a multitude of boils and encrusted injuries, including many bruises. On the right shoulder especially. It shimmered in the most adventurous colors. As a right-hander, I had always put the twelve-kilogram MG on my right shoulder. It seemed to have caused my shoulder to be lowered slightly in the past months. Since my comrades were in a similar condition, the paramedics issued special ointments. When smeared on the most purulent boils, they made them disappear after a week or two. Food was richly distributed. Meat soup, boiled potatoes, and even wine. We could fill up as often as we wanted. Sometimes, the Landser almost drove the chef of the field kitchen to despair. I, too, lined up several times at every meal like a hungry, chirping chick. Military duties were limited to the bare minimum. Weapon cleaning, inspections, and some guard duties within the village alternated with extended periods of rest. All this revived our spirits. We were able to exchange our worn clothes for new ones. On that occasion I managed to get hold of a new pair of field trousers and a new camouflage jacket with a wide hood. The jacket was brown on the outside and light grey on the inside so you could turn it inside out in winter. Stitched on the front were some buttoned pockets in which I stowed my essential belongings. These included a folding knife, matches, and of course bread, rusks, and other food rations. Finally, I also got a new pair of mountain boots. My father's advice to always get a pair one size larger so I could put on a second pair of socks was upheld throughout the war. This way I never had to struggle with frostbite on my toes.

In addition to the replenishment of equipment and weapons, in early May two more marching battalions arrived from home. These were the battalions of 3 GD Numbers 16 and 17, each with a size of about one thousand men. The heavily damaged regimental sections could, therefore, be replenished to some extent. Our platoon received some replacements and several brand-new MG 42s. The platoon command was finally passed on to the East Styrian sergeant, who had handed the company command over to a young lieutenant. During his introduction, he shook hands with everyone and immediately addressed us by our first names, just as you would amongst old Gebirgsjäger. He recognized me and patted me on the shoulder with a big grin. At the same time, all vacationers and some convalescents arrived from home—including the Alsatian. We were overjoyed. And of course he had kept his word and brought some beef jerky and sausages, which we immediately shared with the group. That evening we sat and talked deep into the night. When I told the Alsatian about the terrible hardships of the retreat to the Dniester, his originally joyful expression darkened. It seemed to me that guilt had overcome him. That he had not been there. It may sound paradoxical, but perhaps he thought that he could have gotten some comrades through if he had been with us. In turn, the stories he told from home had also left me somewhat queasy. The area from which he came was indeed influenced by people of German descent, but had been part of France before the war. Like him, many of his contemporaries had volunteered to serve in the Wehrmacht in order to fight against Bolshevism. But when the luck turned, it had visible effects on the mood of his compatriots. There was a passive resistance to the German rulers in some places. Front soldiers were no longer excitedly welcomed upon their return, but dully ignored. He also told me about the fate of a classmate who had gone missing while on leave. Betrayed after a few weeks of hide-and-seek, he was arrested by the security service and executed. Until then I had not heard of such methods on home soil. At best such draconian action corresponded with the difficult situation in which the Third Reich found itself in its fifth year of war. It evidently seemed that achieving "Endsieg" justified any means. This was seconded by deserters dangling from trees, which I saw later during our retreat, when passing through Slovakia.

Equally new were reports about the so-called "bombed-out people." I did not know that the allied bomber offensive was nearing its peak at the time. Whole cities and industrial centers sank into ruins. The bombed-out people were distributed throughout the whole Reich. For this reason, the parents of the Alsatians had taken in two orphans from the Rhineland, whose parents had died in a bombing raid. Inevitably I had to think about my own loved ones. I could not imagine any military impact on a place as sleepy and remote as my East Styrian homeland, however. I could not have been more wrong! The material devastation, deaths, and countless rapes during the Red Army's invasion in April 1945 give a gruesome testimony that nothing and nobody is safe from the war.

But for the time being, I was glad to be back in the circle of old and new comrades. The uninterrupted supply of brand-new weapons, ammunition, and magnificent pack animals did the rest. And once again we saw our own guns, tracked vehicles, and trucks rolling through the village. The division was resurrected, rebuilt around a core of experienced Jäger and leaders that could be relied on by hook or by crook.

After a few weeks of well-deserved rest, 3 GD was once again ordered to the front, this time as part of the 8th Army. We occupied a wide safety line in the foothills of the eastern Carpathian Mountains. At last, a terrain tailored for us

Gebirgsjäger. The Carpathian Mountains stretch out in a large north-facing arc, from Bratislava to the Romanian lowlands. Their peaks reach heights of over 2,500 meters in places. Ever since time began, the Carpathians have been something of a bulwark against the East. Be it the invasions of the Mongols, Tartars, Turks, or the Russians at the time of Tsarist rule. The hills of our new battlefield were covered with magnificently mixed forests, in between large crags from which one could see far into the distance. Narrow muddy roads ran through narrow valleys created by small streams and rivers. The area was sparsely populated. Here and there, small villages. But nature dominated the scenery. Life was largely determined by the forest and livestock industry. Câmpulung on the Moldova was the only major city. It was about 10 kilometers behind the front line and housed not only the regimental staff but also a few supply units and a small hospital.

Immediately after arriving in the Carpathian Mountains, we began to build a chain of bases. The defense section was too long for continuous trenches and we wanted to avoid the mistakes made in the Ukraine, where the thinly occupied defensive lines were broken up all too quickly. Every base was set up as an all-round defense post. Occupied with one or two companies and equipped with grenade launchers and a generous ammunition store. We intended them to be able to hold their own against any enemy onslaught for a long time. The rest would then be done by the reserve troops of the regiment. We dug for weeks. Deep into the earth. Felling trees, building bunkers, and setting wire obstacles. Pioneers sprinkled the whole area with booby traps. The artillery positioned their howitzers in the valley. Out of sight of the enemy but able to fire over our heads as needed. Once our base was finished, we christened it "Graz," a token to the many East Styrians who served in the I. Battalion/ Gebirgsjäger Regiment 138. Other bases were named

"Carinthia," "Danube," or "Stubai." Our MG primary and alternate positions had an excellent line of fire toward the enemy. The terrain was made of shallow hills, until it turned into lowland in the northeast. The Russians could try to attack with tanks but would soon get stuck at the bottom of the valley—that is, if they got that far. An attack would have to be carried out by infantry. And we had always managed to deal with infantry.

The only thing that worried us was the Romanians embedded between the regiments. The German leadership could not do without them during this stage of war, but at the same time, they did not want to have a lone Romanian division be responsible for a front section. Mistrust had been burning all too deeply after the annihilation of the 3rd and 4th Romanian armies in Stalingrad. Hence the mixing. Basically, throughout the months, our relationship with our ally and its population was good. And still we did not envy them because of their backward equipment. Much more difficult was the cohesion of the Romanian units. This proved to be a bit of a disaster. The mostly aristocratic officers lived a life of luxury, even at the front. Yet the simple soldier vegetated away in his hole in the ground. The risk of death and wounding also suffered an unequal distribution. As soon as it got heated, the Romanian commanders were the first to leave. The poor Romanian soldiers had to take up the unequal fight by themselves, only to quickly succumb to death.

We spent June and July 1944 in unusual silence. The fighting was characterized on both sides by extraordinary passivity. Our main focus was on improving food sources and furniture for the shelters. The division kept some cows on the grassy hills of the hinterland. This guaranteed a supply of fresh meat. There was also lively bartering going on with the Romanians. Once a few Romanian soldiers came up to us and offered us a suckling pig for sale. Since we could not spend our pay anywhere else, and the future was still uncertain, we immediately struck a bargain. In absence of more useful kitchen utensils, we boiled the piglet and a sheep that had been brought in later in a large iron bathtub. Both were feasted upon.

The familiar scent of the forest, the forceful nature, and the summery warmth could have almost distracted one from the fact that there was a war going on. Only the sniper was in high demand. Quite often, Landser came over to our ditch carrying scoped rifles and asking about enemy observations. Then they sneaked out into the forecourt and waited for the carelessness of the Russians. If a single shot swept across the no man's land these days, you could be sure that a man was about to breathe his last. Losses by Russian snipers, as far as I remember, were rather rare. We had already learned in Nikopol how to deal with this latent danger. If there was no immediate threat, we let the opponent be, so as not to unnecessarily draw attention to ourselves. Not everyone agreed, however, and the young, inexperienced replacements were much more vulnerable to taking a hit than us "old" Landser. That can be illustrated with the following example.

We were in position, our MG pointed to secure the northeast. Behind us, a handsome boulder, which we used as cover when busy with supply activities. As already mentioned, soon after crossing the Dniester, the company had been taken over by a young lieutenant. He had arrived fresh from war school and thus far had experienced only a few skirmishes against some partisans. In his head was the constant idea of single-handedly turning the tide of war in favor of the Greater German Reich. He permanently had the urge to do something. Or maybe it was just his exaggerated youthful zeal that drove him on. As long as the sergeant or some other experienced senior Jäger was with him, he kept his silly ideas in check. But then, one bright sunny day, he came to inspect our ditch alone. There, he inquired about the enemy's positions. These were quickly pointed out to him across the whole terrain, but of course, the enemy being the enemy, there was no sight of them at all. After all, the Russians were true masters in camouflage. He then ordered me to shoot some salvos at the closest one. I did not want to betray our carefully constructed position, so I hesitated. When he noticed this, he said in a derogatory tone: "Well, what are you waiting for, are you too much of a coward to shoot?"

I heard a restrained "Why don't *you* shoot!" coming from behind. I immediately recognized the voice of the Alsatian, who had grown accustomed to our dialect. And the lieutenant would not be embarrassed in front of us. Without further ado, he got a carbine, climbed onto the boulder and fired across to the other side. He did not have a chance to fire a second shot. What was probably a sniper's bullet pierced his left shoulder and threw him off the rock. There he was. With a pained face. Dazed, but alive. A Jäger ran over to him immediately and began to bandage his shoulder. The lieutenant stared in disbelief at his shattered shoulder joint and with the next onset of pain he finally fainted. For him the war was over. Whether he wanted it or not. Only a reckless fool like him would have huge luck like that. At least that was what we thought at the time. The sergeant came running over a little later, and, soon realizing what was going on, he accused the Alsatian, the most experienced of the group, of not exercising his "duty of care."

"I do not care if the boy is an idiot, only that he will be missing when the Russians march again." Those were his admonishing words.

We did not think much of it. To us, it was just another small episode in a big war. In addition to that, our carefully constructed entrenchments would take a bit of work to invade. "Marching" alone would not chase us down the ridge.

The Russians would have to take a different tack.

Some of the things we Landser saw coming, and others, like the trouble brewing in Romania in the late summer of 1944, we did not. Our supposedly peaceful days were coming to an end. The weak Russian rifle divisions opposite us had silently been replaced by guard units. Fresh, rested, and bent on getting their own back on the Germans. The tragedy's second act was about to begin.

CHAPTER 6

ALL FALLING APART IN ROMANIA

On August 9 at 8 a.m., the entry in my pocket diary says: "Heavy barrage for the past two hours. Everyone is squatting in the bunker." We all sat tightly pressed together in our sleeping quarters. Sand dust trickled from the bunker ceiling with each impact nearby. Conversations were out of the question. The storm of destruction raging over our heads was much too loud. Some of the young Landser were trembling incessantly. The Alsatian, on the other hand, sat there with a determined expression. His jaw clenched as if he were biting on something hard. He glanced over to me from time to time, nodding slightly.

I had already checked the MG for the tenth time—opened the lid and the feeder top and then let the shutter slide back and forth slowly. I had also been through the ammo boxes to make sure the cartridges were properly positioned in their clamps. Looking at the lips of a comrade, I saw him mumbling a prayer: "Jesus, Mary, full of grace ..." Each time there was a pause our heads went up, only to flinch again with the next artillery strike. I do not remember how long this artillery fire lasted. One thing was certain, however: the Russians were not firing grenades just for fun. They would attack very soon. But where?

The barrage ended as abruptly as it had begun. The Alsatian was first out of the bunker. I followed close behind, the MG in my hand. The smoke of corrosive sulfur took our sight and breath. The area around the base was littered with shredded and fallen trees. Landser poured out of the earth like ants out of an anthill and moved to their assigned positions. But getting there proved to be something of an obstacle course. Over tree trunks, through craters, across boulders blasted to smithereens. The adrenaline rush and the destruction were disorienting. And then, there it was again: that hissing sound close by. Infantry fire! The enemy had arrived. Without being able to make out where they were, I set up the MG and sent out harassing fire first. We heard Russian commands. These were followed by a loud whistling and a throaty roar: "Charge!" Seeing the waves of enemy lines storming toward us, I automatically went back into war mode. Swinging the MG from side to side, I stopped the human figures wherever they showed themselves. But the Russians got closer to our positions with every leap, using the trees and rocks as cover. Grenades flew. There was a rush of glowing shards of iron that ate inexorably through skin and flesh. We had already suffered the first casualties. Calls for the paramedics grew louder and louder. Where one comrade fell, his neighbor immediately took his place and carried on firing. Not long now and the enemy would break into the base. The attack waves seemed never-ending. The Alsatian pulled his spade out of his belt and placed it next to the MG. Then he loaded the next belt.

Suddenly, a deafening thud, and the soil flew up around us. Instinctively I pulled the MG back into the ditch. The ground shook as if the world was going down. Friendly fire? The grenades that struck the remaining treetops turned their summerly splendor into deadly wood splinters. We pushed ourselves under the overhang of a ragged rootstock, all body parts drawn in like a turtle's neck. The place was literally raining with stones and splinters. Salvo after salvo struck the forest with a terrible roar. The wall of fire started moving down the slope, slowly but noticeably. I glanced cautiously up to look for the enemy. It was as if he had been swallowed up by the ground. This happened again and again, and when a stray grenade struck nearby, I crept back under the rootstock.

Over there! A figure in an earth-brown uniform standing between two trees. No more than 80 meters away. He had no weapon, his head was bowed, and he seemed dazed. The next moment he disappeared in the clouds of a lightning blast. Once the smoke cleared, the figure had disappeared completely. On the bare-swept branches hung the remains of what had once been a human being.

The attack had been averted. At least for now. Our comrades from the artillery had saved us from a serious close-combat situation. But there was no rest for the wicked. Angry at their own misgivings, the Russians responded with heavy calibers. Even though everyone had managed to get back to the bunker, it wasn't until nighttime that we could carry off the dead and the wounded and replenish our ammunition. Losses had been minimal, despite the heavy bombing. The painstaking trench work had been worthwhile. Nevertheless, the sergeant warned the night guard to be extra vigilant. For there was nothing left of the booby traps and wire locks. Besides, the enemy had much better knowledge of our positions now.

The next day, the shelling carried on, this time with noticeably less intensity. This was followed by another failed infantry attack. On the other hand, impacts were still to be heard to the northwest. The two mortars of the company shot harassing fire over to the Russian side. But something did not seem quite right. The experienced Landser had a sixth sense for changing "weather conditions." We had no idea what had happened around us. We did not know that the enemy had broken through a Romanian unit bordering the 138th Regiment. We also did not know that some bases were cut off from their backward connections and had to defend themselves in severe combat. As a frontline soldier, one remained in constant uncertainty about such details. Even the platoon leaders were often only able to give information about the immediate situation of the company. The rest had to be pieced together, and one's assumptions were often quite correct.

One morning the intense waiting turned into a hectic bustle. A battlegroup was put together to free the northwestern sector. Our group also volunteered for this. We headed down the valley. We had left the tripod mount but were packed with ammunition. Once in the valley, we were united with other parts of the battalion. In contrast to the fighting in Ukraine, where the leadership orders were given only by rule of thumb, here, an officer issued detailed commands. "1st Platoon follows the lane into staging area X. 2nd Platoon closes off the valley side to the south and moves in at Zulu-time. Closing up at the top of Z." Details of mortar and artillery deployment were also discussed. This reminded me of my time as a recruit. Shortly after our departure, a burst of summer rain set in, soon accompanied by thunderstorms. We were soaked to the skin within minutes. The drenched clothes weighed twice as much and turned the uphill climb into a laborious task. The experienced soldier, however, knew that adverse weather conditions always play in favor of the attacker. Not only do they suppress the sounds of the rattling ammunition boxes and weapons, but they also hinder the defender's view. During good weather, the attacker usually doesn't know where the opponent lies until he opens fire.

Conversely, as defender, one can let the enemy get as close as possible until one's own weapons have the greatest effect. Nature was clearly on our side that day.

Not a word was spoken during the approach. Everyone was waiting. Once in the staging area, we formed a long line. The sergeant sneaked from man to man to check that everything was in order. When he got to us, he briefly stopped and patted the Alsatian and myself on the shoulder. He knew that the MG would do its work, and that we would do the same. I had set the bipod to "medium support." A peculiarity that is unique to German machine guns, and that increases the swivel range. Fast firing in all directions was important, especially during a forest fight. I had put the strap around my neck so I could fire from my hip if necessary. The rain fell heavily onto the mountain cap gathering at the edge of the canopy and then dripped at regular intervals onto the moss-covered ground. I looked at the clock over and over. My eyes fixated on the unstoppable second hand. The movement of the hand made the past few months of almost peaceful life fade away. When not staring at the second hand, I looked at the proud trees. Carpathian primeval forest giants with arm-length diameters. Where would my father start if he wanted to cut them down? What kind of beautiful firewood could you make of them? All questions that were spoken into the wind before the storm began.

The Alsatian's short "Hans, it's starting" brought me back to reality. The Jäger of the left fireteam rose silently from their positions and were submerged in the thick of the forest 20 to 30 meters further on. Then it was our turn. We took large leaps up the forest slope. At the same time, our own grenades drew hissing tracks through the wilderness and detonated far out of sight. That also gave a signal to the Russians. Scattered shots whistled across the terrain. After each change of position, I fired aimlessly into the probable direction of the enemy. It seemed like projectiles rattled down from the treetops. Then an Oberjäger chased a long MP salvo into the branches, and shortly after a Red Army soldier tumbled down.

The intoxicating feeling of attack can only be described by someone who has experienced it. Adrenaline shoots straight to the head. The field of vision narrows to a tunnel. Heart and lungs run at full speed. The whole body is under steam pressure. One concentrates only on very few activities. Run, peek for the next cover, shoot, move, leap, change location. One's sense of time and space is lost. Only a few striking moments burn themselves into one's memory and can still be retrieved after decades: the sergeant shouting at a Landser to move his "damn ass"; the gasping Alsatian beside me, who suddenly had blood running out of his mouth; the hand that I burned while changing the barrel because I did not have time to find the glove. The enemy line only became apparent when I stumbled over the first dead Russian. During the assault, pointed thorns were sticking into my legs. I embraced them as if nature wanted to hold me back to protect me from death. The feeling of being needed by my comrades drove me on. The resistance before us began to abate. Then, suddenly, we heard battle noise raging below us. A Russian counterattack? Unrecognized positions? Without looking back, the sergeant continued to drive our train further up. Once at the top we found only abandoned foxholes. All sorts of weapons and equipment were strewn around. The artillery fire had stopped. Drained, we finally let ourselves fall into the man-deep holes and gave the usual ammunition and medical reports.

Fortunately, my comrade had nothing serious. Looking into his mouth, I realized that he had somehow bitten his tongue and so was spitting blood. Such minor injuries were not even worth mentioning. My hand hurt a lot, but in the end it had just turned a little red. I wrapped it in a wet rag to cool it down. The rain was still pounding the ground with undiminished violence. With our adrenaline decreasing, fatigue set in. My head was a bubble. My throat dry as if I had not drunk for days. Typical symptoms that appeared after each battle. I tilted my head back and with my eyes closed I let the raindrops patter into my mouth. They had the sour taste of sulfur. The painful moan of a wounded man echoed from the forest below until it slowly subsided under the effect of a morphine injection.

We only had a brief rest. Just after dark, we were back on our feet, ready to take the second hill. The attack began at dawn and proceeded in a similar fashion. The rain had stopped. Stubborn resistance was only encountered on the hilltop itself. We had taken a favorable position on a ledge and were able to fire directly over the holes and ditches of the Russians. These fought with the utmost obstinacy and repeatedly threw grenades at us. Just when I thought I had caught one Russian, another steel helmet appeared above the edge of the earth. So the cat-and-mouse game picked up once more. No one wanted to surrender, despite several requests. Finally, a few brave Jäger crawled within a few yards of the foxholes and smoked them out with hand grenades one by one. Scraps of body parts and clothing flew through the air after each detonation. Soon after that, black smoke spilled out of the holes as if they were gateways to hell itself. Above the surreal scenery, a feeling of triumph. We had been victorious. Paid for with just a few seriously and some slightly wounded. At the end of it all, the Russians had not just been wiped out completely, they had also lost all the territory they had gained.

By the time we returned to base, all fatigue had disappeared. Curious as to what had happened, our comrades asked about our experiences of the last two days. They had kept our food rations for us, so we stuffed our bellies with greedy bites. Schnapps was passed around to toast the fortunate outcome of the attack. An old Jäger started a song: *"Auf der Heide blüht ein kleines Blümelein und das heißt Erika ..."* We immediately sang along at the top of our voices. Comrades outdid each other with jubilant yodels. The mood was at its peak. Confidence was fully restored. We would fight our way through everything until the eyes ...

I looked around with a beaming face until I suddenly noticed the outline of our sergeant. Nobody else had noticed his arrival in the shelter yet. His eyes were filled with anger. His lips were pressed tightly together. His hands were clenched into fists, as if he wanted to punch someone right now. Hypnotized, I fixed my eyes on his. One comrade after another did the same. The song ebbed away. After seconds of dead silence, he finally opened his mouth:

"Lads! The Romanians have changed sides, they are fighting against us now. The devil will have them!"

That was it, the party was over—but what had happened in the meantime?

The Russian attack on August 19 had been little more than a diversionary tactic. The main offensive had started soon after in the southern part of the Eastern Front. Despite the intense defense preparations of the Wehrmacht, it only took a few days until the front on the Dniester was completely blown apart in several places. The main reason for this was the complete failure of the Romanian ally. Most of their units had broken away from their positions before the attack had even started. The resulting holes could no longer be filled, and to make matters worse, Hitler's senseless halt orders had an effect on the troop's scope of action. Just as in Stalingrad, Orsha, Minsk, and Bobruisk, whole divisions were doomed and had to endure a hopeless situation. In the meantime, the enemy's mechanized formations could flow unhindered into the rear and cut off all rail and road links. The resulting pocket was then wiped out by the enemy's incoming infantry. In that pincer-like operation, which lasted only from August 20 to 25, 1944, no less than twenty German divisions perished. That meant the loss of more than 250,000 soldiers! And all that at a time when the German Reich to the east had already suffered losses of 400,000 soldiers during the destruction of the Heeresgruppe Mitte in June and July. Matters were not much better at the western front either. At the end of August 1944, after the calamity of Falaise, the destruction of the German 7th Army and 5th Panzer Army recorded the loss of another 200,000 men.

The German defeat at Stalingrad is regarded as the turning point of the war. The failed tank offensive near Kursk in summer 1943 marked the last attempt of the Germans to regain the strategic capacity to act again. The meaning of the summer of 1944, however, is often lost in the soundings of all the familiar battle names. But it was just that summer that cast a dark shadow over the German Landser. The shadow of the final act of war, the naked struggle for survival. Inescapable and marked by a nightmarish madness as only that Moloch, war, can orchestrate.

But what did it mean for us Jäger, who were still hanging on in the East Carpathian Mountains?

The Romanian dictator Antonescu had been overthrown and arrested on August 23. The coup was undertaken by a previously formed opposition bloc and supported by the king. Michael I declared war on Germany just two days later. The second-largest contributor of the Axis powers had changed sides. And this during a phase when the Third Reich encountered hardly any ally loyalty at all. On the contrary, hostile forces moved ever closer to the German heartland. Slowly but surely, the news began to leak through to the troops. The military catastrophe had become inevitable. 3 GD was lucky that it lay on the northern edge of this ever-swirling vortex. For the time being, it had escaped all destruction, unlike the units deployed further to the south. They were up to their necks in it, and that in the truest sense of the word. In the days after the overthrow, the Romanian units gradually dissolved or ran over to the enemy.

The tragic thing was that some parts of our division were subordinated directly to Romanian combat units. Some batteries of the laboriously replenished mountain artillery and parts of our anti-tank battalion, for instance. They all went down during the days of the coup. Only a few soldiers were able to reach us, leaving all their equipment behind. Their tales truly shocked us. The betrayal of the former ally was so deceitful, and in many places characterized by such a brutal bloodlust, that it filled the hearts of many a Jäger with deep hatred. We hacked into the bases we'd been building for weeks, especially after Russian reconnaissance patrols had moved inland. A Romanian squad that had ventured too close to our positions was shot down on the spot. To the last man.

When the sergeant returned from headquarters, he was more uptight than usual. He was talking about a great witch hunt and a completely chaotic situation. We should get ready to go. The bulk of the division was already rolling over the rear passes. I had not even rolled up my mat when the definitive withdrawal order arrived. What else was there to be held on the easternmost tip of the German Eastern Front? There was nothing more to save here. From one day to the next, we found ourselves in hostile territory. Divided into small combat groups, we retreated ever deeper into the Carpathian Mountains and left our well-developed positions once again. The most urgent measure was to keep some of the Carpathian crossings open so that our own troops, especially the slow supply trains and the wounded, could get out safely.

Furthermore, the fleeing military worm was joined by an almost endless stream of Transylvanian Saxon refugees. My war tales would be incomplete if I did not mention the suffering of the civilians and above all the terrible fate of these displaced persons. The soldier had the enemy in front of him and home behind him. With the certainty that the homeland was something worth fighting for. But what about those who had to leave their homes in the face of the Soviets rolling in? For those who stayed behind it was likely that they had to face serious attacks by the "liberators" or, even worse, deportation to Siberia. Stalin's mistrust of all non-Russian ethnic groups was just too great. I had already met thousands of escaped Transnistria Germans upon my arrival in Tiraspol in March 1944. What little they had was loaded onto primitive horse-drawn carts. They always camped near our collection points. Out in the open, mind you. At that time, our supply unit tried its very best to provide them with the essentials they needed. Particularly sad was the fact that the refugees consisted almost exclusively of women, children, and elderly people. There was hardly a young person in sight. With babies wrapped in rags and strapped to the front of their chests, the brave women tried to get through the day as best as they could. Living from hand to mouth, facing an uncertain future. Where should they go? Would they even be able to build a new existence? Their harsh destiny is often lost in the historical reviews of the war years. In addition, many of the young ethnic German men had volunteered to serve in the Waffen-SS, in areas that were once part of Greater Germany. Their self-sacrificing struggle against Bolshevism remained futile. We had long been on the side of the losers.

The desertion of Romania further aggravated the situation for the civilian population. The Romanians themselves were facing the fate of decades of communist rule. Escape was the only way. Especially for the resident Volksdeutsche. So, after August 25, 1944, the former German settlement areas emptied in rapid succession. Bistritz, Sibiu, Schässburg, and

Kronstadt are just a few of the cities that were completely affected by the collapse of the Heeresgruppe South Ukraine. As we left our positions in the Eastern Carpathians, we moved westward through Câmpulung as part of the 8th Jäger Division, closely followed by the slow refugee columns of the Transylvanian Saxons. The 144th Regiment had been detached from the division with the order to march south to fill a wide gap at the front. The ethnic Germans in the Szekler Zipfel had slightly more time. As part of the Second Vienna Diktat, they had been ceded to Hungary in 1940. The Szekler Zipfel was a crescent-shaped arc extending along the north and northeastern border of Transylvania. The population there was half Hungarian, half Romanian. Hurriedly mobilized Hungarian border guards tried to hold the area into September. Looking at these Hungarian troops, it was obvious to us how futile this undertaking was. Old haggard men with dysfunctional weapons, probably leftovers from World War I. I suddenly remembered my father's KuK uniform. These border guards looked like a parade troop from the last Great War. Nice to look at on an old postcard, but the battle-hardened Russian Red Army would sweep over them like a winter storm over decaying trees.

Conditions and orders changed almost daily during these weeks of retreat. One minute we lay behind a railway bridge in platoon-strength in order to secure the work of combat engineers blowing up the bridge; the next minute all available soldiers were used to cut down the trees along a mountain road to hinder the enemy. An utterly useless undertaking, since the Russians had already outstripped us to the left and to the right. Again and again we lost contact with our own troops. Especially when conducting rearguard tasks. We were often only used as an MG group and had to hold out all day. The nocturnal marches to compass bearings were particularly annoying. You never knew who you might bump into in the pale moonlight. Was it one of your own or was it the enemy? All of this caused unnecessary tension, and many a Landser fell victim to friendly fire. It often remained completely quiet for days on end. Not a soul in sight. And then, sudden pressure from the enemy, often so powerful we had to run like rabbits.

I can still remember that morning when our MG group of maybe five or six men had been assigned as the rear guard. The rest of the company was to retreat through a narrow valley. The MG position was at the foot of a hill. Our comrades had dug their foxholes at some distance. The surrounding terrain was difficult to walk in. The MG looked straight at a bare slope. Behind it was a dense forest that rose steeply upward. The whole morning had been quiet, when suddenly, at noon, Romanians attacked. An entire battalion! The wildly shouting mob came straight out of the forest. Completely uncoordinated and without any support weapons. The Alsatian had chosen our position with reasonable foresight. The bare slope was like a bottleneck. It was channeling the enemy. You just had to fire enough sheaves to stop them. He let the Romanians come up as far as 200 meters and opened fire at the very last moment. He drove the gun back and forth with mechanical constancy. The high cadence of the weapon did the rest. The first sheaves were already well within aim and had the Romanians dropping straight to the ground. Some of the fallen tumbled down the slope. Probably not expecting such strong resistance, the Romanians stopped after a few meters. Once the first enemy soldier had thrown his gun to the ground and stuck his hands in the air, the others quickly followed. The drama was over just as quickly as it had begun.

There were around two hundred Romanians scattered about with their hands up in the air. Lying amongst them were the dying and wounded, who wallowed in the grass, moaning and groaning. Guns at the ready, I and another comrade started to collect our freshly gained prisoners of war. They were greatly astonished by our little group. They must have expected a considerably larger force. As I approached one group, I recognized a single soldier as he slowly lowered his hand. I immediately shouted at him in broken Romanian, "*Mâinile sus! Mâinile sus!*"—"Hands up!"—but in return he pulled something out of his coat pocket and a single shot broke through the silence. I ducked and the bullet only just missed my head. Still going down, I shot him with my semiautomatic. At almost the same time, the Alsatian was firing the MG into the group. First a scatter directly into the mass, and the last bursts of fire just above the ground. Then, silence. I screamed "*Mâinile sus!*" once more. The first soldiers rose reluctantly from the ground. The screaming of the wounded had intensified. Having gotten over the initial shock, I started waving the Romanians backward one at a time. They were thoroughly searched under the watchful eye of gunner 1 and then arranged in a long line. Some were wounded. Many had tears in their eyes and their heads hung low. My compassion was limited. I could not afford to have humanitarian feelings in the presence of the ubiquitous danger of death.

We saw our rearguard order as fulfilled. Apart from that, we were not supposed to wait for the arrival of additional enemy units. So we moved back down into the valley and met up with the company by the late afternoon. The severely wounded and dead remained on the battlefield. Just like the many weapons scattered in the grass. Who could have taken care of them during such a turbulent situation? The company received us with dropped jaws—we had taken so many prisoners! The sergeant was especially happy about the success, and saw his personal account with the Romanians as settled.

"Well done, guys, great! The devil never sleeps!"

A few days later, I and another comrade received the Iron Cross 2nd class for our part in this victory. The Alsatian had already received one ages ago and during a short roll call was awarded the Iron Cross 1st class. Then, life rolled on. But our losses grew too, and our combat strength shrank noticeably. Following the course of the Tesna, we marched further back to the west via Borsa. We were told to aim for Hungary. At least for now. But that did not happen.

The situation on the Hungarian border, and also that of some of the Hungarian units, who had changed their priorities, made us change our plans. We made for the Romanian-Polish border at the great junction of Moissei, to be precise. There we were intercepted by German military police and sent toward the Romanian heartland. The whole company was moved onto columns of waiting trucks and driven south all through the night. Tightly wedged between the warm shoulders of two comrades at the sides and the monotonous shaking of the truck behind and below, I fell asleep immediately. The next morning, we found ourselves at the station of Deda. Everything had gathered here. From construction engineers to supply troops, and even some members of the Luftwaffe. There was a distinct feeling of improvisation in the air. Watching some staff officers running back and forth nervously did not make the situation any better. After a short roll call, we took over some of the front sections that had been abandoned by the Hungarian border units. The ascent to the mountain ridges, quite a few of them over 1,000 meters high, turned out to be an exhausting ordeal—especially with a tripod mount and ammunition on your back. The former Hungarian positions could only be made out by their extinct fireplaces and empty cans. They had not even dug any foxholes before they had defected to the enemy.

"If we all would have defended our homeland as well as the Hungarians and Romanians, the war would have been over a long time ago," remarked the Alsatian laconically. This was only partially true. Admittedly, my early experiences with the Hungarians had left a bad impression. But I had only seen their third-rate troops so far. Later in the Hungarian lowlands, near Budapest and at Lake Balaton, their regular troops defended themselves right down to the last man. Some of their army and air force contingents continued to fight on Austrian soil even when everything was already lost. A fact that often gets forgotten in favor of the loud tales of German battle prowess.

We did not have to wait around for very long until first enemy contact. The Russian infantry had slowly marched up the forest slope by the next morning, probably to occupy the mountain ridge. "Inexperienced troops," I thought. We had used the time to make ourselves invisible. The MG was hidden in the wide trough we had dug and was covered up with fir branches. As usual during a forest fight, the MG rested on the bipod set to medium support. I had deposited the tripod down by my feet, well wrapped in tarpaulin. I really did not want to have to clean the mud off it after each downpour. A Landser's few possessions, if one could call them that, were always on them or in the mountain rucksack. If it was necessary to pack up quickly it would only take a few seconds and we would be ready to march again. On top of my backpack were five to six hundred rounds of ammunition, tucked away in two or three long straps. The classic ammo boxes were very unpopular with us Jäger. First of all, they clanged like crazy. Secondly, their weight pulled your arms down like rubber hoses. Having the belts in the backpack made them much easier to carry and eliminated the noise. If required the individual MG straps could simply be hung together on an empty linkage while they rattled through the MG. This method had proved perfect time and again, especially because of the barely noticeable breaks while firing. Due to the high cadence of the MG 42—an incredible twenty-five rounds per second—gunner 1 had to understand his craft well. First and foremost, good housekeeping with the ammunition was imperative. Precise, short bursts of fire were the means of choice to inflict the greatest possible damage on the enemy. Apart from that, the devil was in the details. Any signs of excavation were dumped further back, so as not to leave any signs of human activity. The forest had to look untouched. Any camouflage material was cut from the trees further back. The sergeant had issued an absolute ban on smoking and fire, for in a forest you can smell smoke long before you can see its place of origin. Nothing should show we were ready to defend. Remaining totally motionless in a position requires great discipline—discipline based on the experience that the element of surprise, whether it is in an attack or defense, can mean the difference between life and death. The motto was "lie like dead meat." Hardly a word was spoken, and when it was, it was whispered. You could only do a number two at night. A fist-like hollow on an earth wall was quite sufficient for the small emergencies in life. One which you could pee in while lying on your side. The black forest soil sucked up the urine and would neutralize its smell immediately.

We let the enemy approach to a few meters' distance, as we had done dozens of times before. Using the serenity of the forest in our favor. You could hear the birds singing in the calm and quiet nature around you. The sharp breaking of dry branches and the suppressed rattling of human lungs, however, betrayed what belonged to the forest and what did not. I perceived the Red Army men here as walking dead. Of course, their souls were still in their bodies. But their fate had long since been sealed. The Russian closest to us suddenly stopped. Almost as if he had known that something was up. One could notice his tired limps from the difficult ascent. He lowered his cap almost delicately and wiped the thick beads of sweat from his forehead. As he looked down on us, his bald shaven head burst under the brutal force of the first sheaf. All hell broke loose. Infernal noise with bitter consequences for the other side. What remained after our sudden outburst of fire either lay stretched out on the forest floor or had disappeared in panic into the thickets. Many a body on the forest floor twitched on for minutes, as if they did not want to acknowledge the irrevocable tragedy. Human blood trickled into the forest soil. Once the powder smoke had cleared, the birds began to sing again as if nothing had happened. Further down the slope we heard the eerie, shrill cries for help of a seriously wounded man.

"*Pomosh, towarish, pomosh!*"—"Help, mate!" But he called in vain. Almost all night. Shaking one's nerves to the core and destroying every thought of sleep.

Inevitably, the question will arise why none of us Jäger had made the effort to come to the aid of the apparently doomed? To explain this, it requires a ruthless disclosure of the facts that prevailed in the East. The fight on the Eastern Front was unlike any other theater of war. Let's make this clear. Death was all around. However, the total brutality with which the two inhumane systems fought on the Russian front is still unparalleled in modern history. In addition, we were driven to these extremes by new weapons technology and the endeavor to totally extinguish the competing system. The German word "Vernichtungskrieg" (war of annihilation) sums this up perfectly. No less striking was the motto to conquer "Lebensraum" (new living space) in the East. From the Russian point of view however, the period from 1941 to 1945 is considered as the "Great Patriotic War," during the course of which the German aggressor was crushingly defeated and expelled from the homeland. The fact that the geostrategic goals of communism were unsatisfied by this was shown during the Cold War between East and West that appeared shortly after and dragged on for many decades. With the common soldier in the eye of the storm. He had to pay for the megalomania of the warlocks. The urge to survive dictated the choice of his means. I had already heard about the severity of the fighting on the Eastern Front whilst in training. An impression undoubtedly distorted by the heroic diction of our own propaganda. The true face of the eastern war revealed itself upon my arrival in Nikopol. Within the first few days of my arrival I had witnessed how two Landser, driven by humanistic sentiment, slipped into no man's land at night to bring in a supposedly wounded Russian. He too had screamed for help. But the comrades did not come back. Such experiences grew more common in the months that followed. Thus, even the last thought of a fair and chivalrous war faded visibly. That was our reality. If otherwise worthless, it can at least serve as a reminder for future generations.

On September 29, 1944, I noted the word "fever" into my pocket diary. The long rainy autumn days and the cool temperatures on the ridge left me in a bad way. Without permanent accommodation, it was completely out of the question that this would improve. Then, one day, while I was bending over under the pain, the sergeant recognized the gravity of the situation. That very same evening I was taken back to the battalion with the supply run. My lips were shaking so hard I could barely speak. The medical center was located in a converted peasant hut. There, I was given antipyretic medication and later transported on by one of the covered vehicles of the supply column. I cannot say how long this went on for, as most of the time I was lost in a deep sleep.

A paramedic looked in on me now and then and brought me some hot soup. Afterward, I immediately crept back into the mobile straw bed with a pleasantly warm feeling in my stomach.

As soon as I was reasonably well rested, I got an assignment to provide the fighting troops with food. For this, we had a horse and cart. I should be able to recover fully under this "light duty." I did not take me long to realize that this was more like a suicide mission on the ever-changing front. By my side was an old Styrian Landser. On the first night it was so dark that we could not find our own troops. So we had to return to the supply train without any results. The next day we decided to leave a little earlier. As the forest path was soon too overgrown, we moved to a dry stream bed. Our horse and cart made a great deal of noise on the dried-out gravel. Unbeknown to us, we had entered into hostile territory. As we turned a bend, we suddenly set eyes on some smoking and chatting soldiers. I thought they were Romanians. Some distance away from them they had stacked their weapons in a pyramid shape. Surprised as both parties obviously were, any hostile action was out of the question. I just raised my hand, said, "Evening," and carried on. My comrade followed me without batting an eyelid. After a few meters, once safely back in the forest, we hurried on. Apparently, the enemy had confused us with their own supply team. Maybe they had also been too tired to go after us. We finally found our own company and reported to them immediately about the unwanted venture into enemy territory.

After this unpleasant experience, I feigned my perfect recovery and was sent back to my MG group. From then on, the supply units enjoyed my highest respect. Their service was not exactly a walk in the park, especially in times of retreat. Logistics is held hostage by warfare. At least to a certain extent. That was already the case at the time of Alexander the Great. The best army in the world cannot exist without ongoing care. And that care was no menial task. Nocturnal marches on unknown paths, mostly alone and with valuable cargo, the rapid removal of wounded or sick soldiers, and of course the repair of weapons and equipment.

There was a joyful welcome upon my return to my unit. Not only because the MG group represented something like a community of lot, but also because there was another body to take on some guard duties. Distress and misery are known to fuse together. Everything was shared: the worries and doubts, the meager rations, and sometimes even a little joke or two. In time, and in the long hours spent together down in the bunker, you got to know your comrades better than your own brother. There is this bond that every frontline soldier knows but cannot explain, and it's braided in countless firestorms, consolidated during the quiet endurance of never-ending suffering that becomes the new way of life. I often thought about my comrades after the war, especially those who fell or went missing. The long winter months on the family farm gave me plenty of time to ponder. I am still convinced that I will see them again. If not in this life, then in the next. The time will come.

But in October 1944 there was no time for such profound thoughts. There were far too many hairy situations. Take October 15, 1944. The Sunday that some Russian gave me my first injury. As already mentioned, we moved mainly at night; the day belonged to the enemy. While we endured long days in lonely mountain dugouts, one of us had to go back to the company headquarters to collect the food for the other comrades at the front. This was mostly done under the cover of darkness. That day it was my turn. So I grabbed my rifle and put the mountain rucksack on my back. I found my way to the issuing office without any problems and immediately returned. Back at our hole, I reached with my right hand to my rucksack to take the loaves. That very second, a single rifle shot whipped across from the enemy's side and brushed my right forefinger. I was rooted to the ground. The Alsatian managed to pull me into the protective hole just before a second shot tore through the silence. With a practiced grip, he fumbled a bandage out of his anorak and dressed the severely bleeding wound. Then he got up and sent a few wild bursts of fire in the direction of the enemy. It is strange what shock does to you. I did not feel anything at all for the first few minutes. Then I suddenly thought my hand would fall off. The pain went through my whole body. I gazed at the bandage under the shimmering moon. It had already turned into a bloody lump. I wanted to cut my finger off just to get rid of the pain. Sleep was out of the question now. So, for the next twenty-three hours, I hung around, unable to do much. The only relief was provided by a cigarette the Alsatian had given me. His last one, too. I had never smoked before. I haven't touched a cigarette since. But the nicotine had a somewhat calming effect. At least for a few minutes.

 The following evening, I had the wound inspected at the medical collection point. The candlelight revealed that the projectile had taken my fingertip off right down to the bone. The fingernail was slightly bent and bloodshot. The flesh was already covered with a weeping crust. I got a tetanus injection into the buttocks because of the risk of gangrene. The paramedic was not exactly gentle, so my backside hurt for days afterward. The wound was not severe enough to stay with the supply train or another rear unit. The front in the Szekler tip was hopelessly overstretched, and every available Landser was needed for its defense. I was told to march back to my platoon that very same evening, sporting a thick bandage around my finger. I was still able to shoot the MG as there was a big trigger on the right side of the tripod mount.

In addition, the depth fire device was operated with the left hand anyway. It was only the belt cartridges that I couldn't properly link together. But there were comrades for that.

By now we had come close to the Hungarian border. Once again, we enjoyed a few days of peace in permanent accommodation. Here we not only supplemented our equipment and ammunition, we also loaded some of those who had recovered from injury off the trains. Their gloomy stories from home made me think. The Americans had already advanced to the Siegfried Line. The Russians had moved deep into Poland. Bombing raids had spread throughout the Reich. Destruction was reported from Vienna, Wiener Neustadt, Graz, and Klagenfurt. Why did our air force, the Luftwaffe, not do anything about it? Surely it could not just be due to having to support the hard-fought remnants of the former Army Group South Ukraine. The Luftwaffe aircraft that had appeared in the sky could be counted on one hand. Besides, they were lucky not to be bombing their own troops in the turmoil of the retreat. By contrast, the Soviets deployed their fighter pilots almost every day. They repeatedly disturbed the rear supply lines, bombed trains, and attacked transport columns. Often with devastating consequences for soldiers and civilians. So who would be surprised that due to the ever-worsening situation, the simple Landser sometimes sought his peace of mind in alcohol? I too grabbed a bucket one night and filled it with half-fermented red wine I had found in a Romanian cellar. The local farmer caught me but did not say anything. Technically, this was looting. I was well aware of the punishment by the Wehrmacht that would have been awaiting me. But who should implement it in this situation? At the time I thought it was madness to compare the theft of some wine with what I had done countless times with my machine gun. One was a crime under the purview of military justice. The other was rewarded with medals. Where was the proportionality, if there was such a thing? I just wanted to forget what had happened and not be reminded of what might come next.

Back at the digs, we had a good old German booze-up. Without encouraging jokes or joyous singing. Faces were grim. The atmosphere was worse than a funeral. Many a Jäger vented his anger and cursed loudly at the "bastards up there." The ones who had thought it all up in the first place. Soldiers who had returned from leave had repeatedly reported about the shabby behavior of the Nazi officials at home. That made my blood boil even more. There were evidently enough of them who, in their over-zealous ideological delusions, had attracted the hatred of their own compatriots. The list of misdeeds was correspondingly long. Persecution of political opponents, making money off the backs of workers and peasants, even the fanatical enforcement of draconian rules that governed normal citizens' everyday economic lives. Many an indispensable farmer had found himself at the front, just because he had slaughtered a pig too many. This of course increased aversion to the Nazi apparatus and fueled vengeful thoughts.

But we made a decision that night: once back home, we had a score to settle with all the bigwigs and warmongers. With a bare blade in our hand, if that was what it took. Just like we had learned at the Eastern Front. Only the sergeant retained his composure.

"Keep your anger for the Russians," he said. "We need to get home first."

He was right, of course. Two out of three of us would never see our beloved homes again.

Our arrival at the Hungarian border marked an end to the fighting on Romanian soil. The retreat was rapid in the days after my minor injury—so rapid I did not even have the chance to note the respective place names into my pocket diary. This time we had ample transport available, not like it had been in Ukraine. Brand-new three-axle trucks with large cargo areas. This saved many miles of walking and allowed us to recover. But there was some reluctance to leave the beautiful Carpathian Mountains behind us. Against all odds, they had brought us luck, those densely forested mountain areas with their many rivers and narrow ravines where the enemy had not been able to exploit their material superiority. Tanks had been largely ineffective on the narrow and winding mountain passes, mainly due to their flat trajectories. The same applied to the enemy artillery. The guns could only shoot at a top angle and were therefore of limited range. So, it was only their mortars that we had to fear. I cannot explain why the Russians had such excellent mortar crews. In any case, they often only needed three or four shots to score a direct hit. Then the only thing left for us to do was to quickly change position.

As far as enemy infantry was concerned, we had always managed to keep them at a distance, even when outnumbered. The MG was made for that purpose. Well-buried and camouflaged, we had often taken on far superior forces, only to disappear silently after a mission had been fulfilled. Such a prolonged fight was blood-saving, as you might say, and thus, in October 1944, the 3rd Gebirgsjäger Division was one of the very few units that arrived in the Hungarian lowlands reasonably intact. There we would face new difficult tasks.

Intimidated by the heavy losses in the Carpathian Mountains, the Soviet leadership had shifted their focus to the lowlands east of the Tisza. It was the end of September when dramatic battles took place around Szolnok, Debrecen, and Nyíregyháza while we were still sitting on the trucks. The latter place was about to turn the fates of many comrades. There, death would confront me once again. This time with full force and the element of surprise.

CHAPTER 7
UNLUCKY IN HUNGARY

The Hungarian Puszta. A tank terrain in the truest sense of the word! We came from the Carpathian foothills at high speed and were swallowed up by the flat, unforested steppe after just a few kilometers. The date was October 23, 1944. We had already passed the stretched Wehrmacht columns and the endless stream of fleeing civilians. Each fork in the road was occupied by military police. Given the turbulent front situation, they waved us through everywhere and anywhere. Their aim was to get us to our new base of operation as quickly as possible. Something was burning, somewhere close. We could feel that even from our truck beds.

The closer we got to the columns of smoke and the dull explosions in the distance, the more silent the Jäger grew. Before we knew it, we were looking into the mouth of a German assault gun that was securing the road. After a brief conversation with the combat commander in charge, our column turned sharply northwest. Soon we arrived at the village of Nagykálló. The village sign was riddled with bullets. The village itself was in a pitiful state. Many of the buildings had been burned down to their foundations, others halfway down. Russian tanks were scattered all around. In between lay heaps of fallen Red Army soldiers and tons of destroyed war equipment. As it turned out, a Soviet attack group—Hussars, so it was said—had taken Nagykálló and the surrounding farming villages a few days earlier and had then advanced further north. An improvised counterattack of a German tank division, which had included the sentry at the entrance of the village, had brought it back into German hands. The Soviet leaders were surrounded, and ran like mad into our defensive positions further up while trying to escape the threat of annihilation. At the time we had no idea that there was an old acquaintance among the enemy units of the front: the IV Guards Cavalry Corps, the unit that had hunted us all the way through Ukraine and almost killed us at the Ingulets. We now had the opportunity to return the favor. Arriving at the main square, we immediately stood on parade, impatiently awaited by a number of senior tank officers. This was followed by a short briefing for the companies of our I. Battalion/ Gebirgsjäger Regiment 138. We didn't quite grasp the details, but half an hour later, as we marched out to the south of the village and across the adjacent fields to take over the line secured by the Panzergrenadierkompanie, it suddenly became clear what was expected: we were to relieve the tank unit, to free them up for further offensive tasks and for securing the enclosure ring to the south. The Panzergrenadiers (mechanized infantrymen) had been in combat for many days, but nonetheless they made a dogged impression. Many were equipped with a new kind of assault rifle. So there must be some truth to the stories of the new miracle weapons. To everyone's surprise, they also gave us some crates of American canned meat they had captured in Nagykálló. This raised our spirits. With such brothers in arms by your side, you could look the Russian steamroller straight in the eye.

We spent the day fortifying our positions. One group

moved into a small wooded area a few hundred meters ahead. They were to protect us from unwanted surprises. Even the Hungarian villagers were eager to help. The brief Russian invasion of the village had devastated the people. The Russians' destructive work did not just affect the Hungarians' material possessions; much worse was what they had done to many of the women and girls. We had already heard reports of mass rape. In one house, a dozen Red Army men had assaulted both mother and daughter. During our brief march through the village, I did see several dead civilians. They had been put on makeshift stretchers and covered with white sheets. Unlike with fallen comrades, where the tarpaulins used to wrap them up were quickly soaked in blood, all the sheets used here were still snow-white. Many of them had women's shoes sticking out over the stretcher. Beside the stretchers, rows of grieving friends and relatives kneeled on the floor. I shuddered at the sight. This incident in the village was a heinous crime against the innocent, which gave the bottomless misdeeds of the Eastern War an additional cruel facet. No wonder the men of the village saw our task as their own.

One of these men used a plow to pull broad furrows into the soil. We then dug on to fashion knee-high connecting trenches. This one Hungarian was so eager to get on with the job that the draft horses almost collapsed under the blows of his whip. On top of that we rushed to expand the pre-dug foxholes into a makeshift position system. There was not enough time for much more. I set the MG up around 50 meters behind the first line, just behind a small rise which should have protected us from direct fire. Slanting away from this rise was a deep field drain leading to the edge of the village. Although filled with water, it would serve as a sheltered retreat, just in case. To the right, within sight, lay the second MG. The company's mortars had taken up position around the village square. A Hungarian woman arrived at our L-shaped hole just before dusk. She had brought fresh donuts. I was deeply touched by the unexpected hospitality and thanked her for the delicious titbits. What must she have thought of us young boys? She was a little older and probably also had sons somewhere in this war. Nagykálló was her home. She would lay all her hopes on us to protect her and her compatriots from the onset of the Red Army. From the hordes of barbarians who had ravaged her village yesterday. Although one or the other Jäger might have actually had this thought, our objective went much further. First of all, we wanted to get out of this catastrophic war. Secondly, Hungary was just the prelude to our beloved homeland. We, I, did not want to let loved ones at home suffer the same fate. Inevitably I had to think of my two sisters. They had just turned sixteen and seventeen. What if the enemy also reached East Styria? It didn't bear thinking about. I looked grimly at the dim light while the first few raindrops began pelting down on my mountain cap. "Russian weather," I thought. "Bring it on."

Rolled up in my tarpaulin I had a quick doze. A thin stream of water ran down my cheek and was absorbed by my scarf. Tangled scraps of dreams floated through my mind. I could see my father standing in front of our burning house. The tear-soaked eyes of my mother. Earth-brown figures walking up the steep slope. And I was standing right next to them, petrified.

Bang. I got up immediately, eyes wide awake. Where had that come from? *Bang.* There, another, followed by the dull rumble of a grenade explosion. A desperate cry. Staccato machine-gun fire. There was something going on in the forest, no doubt about it. It was about 300 to 400 meters away. That was where the forward post was situated. Our positions sprang to life. I could even detect activity in the village. The Jäger were probably hurrying to their grenade launchers, taking the grenades from their container and preparing the propellants. The battle noise exploded once again, until there was a sudden deadly silence.

After what seemed half an eternity, I heard a suppressed "Parole?" from the foremost rifle holes. Then, nothing. Suddenly, the ghostly contours of a stooping, limping figure appeared from the darkness.

The Alsatian sprang into action: "Parole? Dammit comrade, parole!?"

"Odessa."

"Come in."

Before I knew it, a Jäger dropped into our MG position. He was struggling for breath, mumbling fragments of words: "Did not see them coming. Hear them either. They were suddenly there. Took us all out, one after the other."

I fixated on his trembling lips. My hands clenched to fists, my dirty fingernails digging into my palms.

"Defended ourselves best we could. My thigh was hit. Need to see the medic ..."

I could almost smell the cold blood. The taste of copper on my tongue.

"There. Get into the drainage, it will lead you through to the house. Ours are there."

Our shocked comrade pulled himself up almost mechanically, and after a few limping steps he had disappeared into the black night. It was only the loud splash of the water-filled ditch that gave witness to the last survivor of a group of Jäger that had fought back with dwindling forces.

"Holy shit! Does this ever end?"

I answered the Alsatian's rhetorical question with a shake of my head.

By now the tiredness was clearly gone. This was not the best start on Hungarian soil. And misfortune, according to my experience of the land, usually attracted more of its kind. Hours later, the sergeant arrived at our position, soaking wet and covered in mud. We had to be careful as hell. He had the feeling that the ones on the other side were not just cannon fodder; they were hardy veterans. Holding my shoulder, he said:

"Go across and take over the other MG. The new replacements are far too nervous for my liking. I cannot rely on them."

I got up reluctantly. By the time I got there, I was also covered from top to bottom in mud. Grumpily, I gave the three guys crouching in their position a few instructions. Above all they were not to shoot until I had opened fire. And they were to dig the backward-connecting trench out deeper. I had no desire to put myself on display during an upcoming firefight.

The cannonade began shortly before dawn. At first there were only isolated shots into the area with mortars. They were answered by sporadic counterfire on our part. *Plop—plop—plop*. Our own shells flew over our heads. Sometimes into the forest. Sometimes a bit further, in the direction of a small cluster of farmhouses. Infantry fire also hissed slowly along. Long, untargeted MG salvos. I could not make out their origin and remained calm for the time being. Then one of the kids detected movement in the forest. Without thinking, he straightened up and fired a few pointless carbine shots in that direction. I shouted at him to kindly sit his ass down and stop firing about! But too late. A grenade struck close to the ditch with thundering force. I had not even heard it being launched. "Damn Russians!" The second grenade was a direct hit. The shredded body of the Jäger flew through the air and fell into the soggy morass. The enemy had recognized our position and methodically peppered it with shells. Coming closer to the MG nest with each and every hit. The way it plowed into the ground, it looked like a gigantic greedy earthworm was coming toward us. The boys that had previously crouched around the MG were in shock.

"Out!" I shouted. "Get out. Get the hell out!" And I pushed the two Jäger backward into the connection trench. After that I threw myself between the sheltering earthworks. Without taking the MG. I crawled through the mud on all fours. Lumps of earth pelted down on me with every impact nearby. One was so close that my mountain cap flew off my head. I left it there and carried on crawling. The two men in front of me suddenly stopped. I ventured to straighten myself up for just a moment and saw the mess. Five meters ahead, the ditch was about to merge into flat farmland. "These damn idiots." They had not extended the ditch to the edge of the village as instructed. And now there was a prize to pay for their laziness. The gun mount came crashing to the ground next to me. Destroyed. The MG nest was gone. I shouted at the men that they should jump, one after the other, to reach the safe edge of the village. But they hesitated. The artillery impacts were coming closer and closer. I jumped to my feet at the very last moment and hurried out into the plain, zigzagging like a hare pursued by a pack of snarling wolves. Waiting for an MG salvo to tear my feet from under my body. But it found another prey: the person hurrying after me. I let myself fall to the ground once again. I stopped for a moment to get ready for one last jump. 30 meters later I rolled off a wall and dropped into a cellar hole. When I looked up, I found myself staring into half a dozen rifle barrels. "Do not shoot! German!" The surrounding Landser lowered their weapons immediately. One handed me a sip of something strong. The liquid burned down my throat. I waited in vain for the rest of the MG crew. The only thing that came in through the basement window was the stink of sulfur.

While I waited in that cellar with some bearded Oberjäger

incessantly barking into the field telephone, a strange feeling suddenly came over me: guilt, and a haunting self-doubt. I had failed. The young comrades had been entrusted to me, although I was probably only one to two years older than them. That did not matter. I had served at the front continuously for over a year now and knew which way the wind blew. The sergeant had given me the order to take over the MG. Now three men were most likely dead. We would only be able to recover shreds of their bodies—if we would find them at all in the rutted soil. I should have kept them closer to me. Above all, I should have checked the connection trench. The inexperienced replacements were not to blame. And all of this dawned on me gradually. Three lads in the prime of their lives. Three families. Mothers, fathers, sisters, and brothers. What a disaster! With the Schnapps came melancholy. I collapsed and began to bawl like a baby. Holding my hands in front of my face to avoid seeing the reactions of the surrounding Landser. Someone gripped my shoulders and pressed me tight against a soft quilted camouflage jacket.

"Everything will be fine, comrade. The assault guns are already rolling outside. We will get our own back."

I felt the ground vibrating. I heard the steady clank of tank tracks. The shrill squeal of the steering maneuvers followed by the sharp firing of a tank cannon. I switched off my head. I had plenty of practice by now. I barred all the feelings that were obstacles in times of need. I had to get out of the cellar. Back into the ditch. Make up for it ...

This morning skirmish in the southern part of Nagykálló is not even included in the history books. Why should it? Because of the couple of fallen Landser? Because of the two or maybe three Russian PAKs (anti-tank guns) that had been destroyed by our assault guns in a quick counterattack? From a military point of view, the situation was stable. The encirclement held. The fatherland would send a few new replacements, equally carefree and equally endowed with the strong yearning for a long and happy life as the recent dead. On this disastrous autumn day, something broke inside me: the belief that we would finally be able to bring the enemy down. Their impetuous infantry onslaught was one thing. You could handle that if you knew how. But dismissing the Russian soldiers as cannon fodder would have done a gross injustice to their abilities and achievements. There were countless excellent warriors within their ranks. Whole units even, which had also been steeled in the forge of the Eastern Front. And on top of that, since Stalingrad, they had gotten drunk on their many victories. For the Russians, each step forward brought them closer to the final triumph over the hated enemy. But things could not be worse for the German Landser. He was no longer master of all things. His fate and that of his homeland rested solely in the hands of the Allied war machinery, which by now was infiltrating the Reich from all sides.

The great tank battle that had been raging in the Puszta since October 6 was coming to its peak right now. Recognizing the danger of the isolation of the entire German 8th Army, the High Command of the Wehrmacht had used a still reasonably intact Panzer Corps from the area around Budapest. This of course meant exposing the local defense section. The leadership had staked everything on one card. In bold mobile advances, the Russian spearheads were struck and the connection between the German 6th and 8th Armies was restored. For almost three weeks, these brave Panzergrenadiers had fought from village to village. With changing priorities at all times. Wherever they went, the enemy suffered heavy material and manpower losses. But at the same time, with every battle, their fighting strength steadily decreased. The few available tanks and grenadiers were grouped into ever-new battle groups. They were asked to achieve the impossible. To make matters worse, on October 15, the Hungarian Governor Horthy had already taken up ceasefire negotiations with the Red Army. The sudden absence of the former ally and thus the total collapse of the Hungarian front was prevented at the very last moment by commando units of the Waffen-SS. Tactically responsible was the notorious SS-Obersturmbannführer Otto Skorzeny. Born in Vienna, he had made a name for himself in September 1943 during the Mussolini liberation. By the end of the war, he was known as Europe's most dangerous man. On October 26, 1944, and with favorable political conditions backing the Wehrmacht High Command up, a final blow was to be made against the trapped Russian cavalry corps. With its annihilation, the German leadership hoped to bring peace to this hard-won front.

By early morning, we knew we were due to attack that day. All sorts of divisional parts gathered in the village. More tracked vehicles and artillery had been brought in. Our southern positions were noticeably thin. Heavily armed Jäger broke out of their trenches and moved to the edge of the village. Worn-out infantry arrived from the other direction. They did not look like regular combat troops and almost collapsed with exhaustion. Once harassed by the sergeant, they gradually moved into the empty trenches. And what was left of the MG crews after the last three heavy battles was to form the main support unit in an otherwise weak defensive line. I still felt miserable and scribbled that into my pocket diary as mental distraction. My comrade from Alsace felt the same way. The days of mutual encouragement were definitively over.

With the first sunbeams, all movements on our side of the front ground to a halt. The view was relatively clear, even if there was a drizzle. At 0600 hours, isolated shots of the divisional artillery rang for the final attack. My nerves were stretched to breaking point. We had to win this one. The wording of the company command had made that perfectly clear. It seemed to me as if an invisible force had rung the bell for the last round of a boxing match. Two fatigued opponents pushed themselves off their stools one last time and staggered toward each other. Enemy harassing fire struck the field. Countless pieces of shrapnel ate into the small mound in front of the MG position. We kept our heads down as much as possible. Any glance at no man's land could have been our last. After every harmless impact, one almost seemed to be born anew. The roar of tank engines around the homestead destroyed the last illusions that the Russians would leave it at a skirmish. There was too much at stake for them, too. Just as we saw our duty in the destruction of the surrounded enemy, they sought their liberation. In fact, the first armored turrets soon appeared. A German assault gun launched its armor-piercing grenades at them. A duel between steel giants. Just as relentless as the fight of man against man. A dark cloud of smoke marked a lucky hit by the German side. The enemy remained at a distance and increased its artillery fire. After an hour or two, some partly motorized and partly covered columns appeared to our right. Stuffed with soldiers. The Alsatian and I took it in turns looking through the MG's Hensold sight to determine their origin. And there was no doubt. A tall dark Soviet star on a covered wagon provided final certainty. Russians! Trying to escape from our deadly grip. Shaken up by the attack of 3 GD. Heading directly toward its lines. I did not hesitate for a second. With slight pressure on the handwheel handle, I released the locking lever of the height limit. Then a few full turns on the handwheel and the MG muzzle turned slightly upward. *Brrr.* A short burst of fire. Nothing. Quick, another turn. *Brrr.* Again nothing. After the fourth or fifth salvo, the Alsatian, who was on the binoculars, announced: "Hit!" So I had found my aiming point. I quickly set the locking levers to the new depth fire marks and fixed the side limiters. 1,500 meters! A more-than-feasible range for a machine gun on a tripod. After that, it was child's play to send out the short, even sheaves methodically to do their job. I changed aim as soon as a car or truck stopped. Only the American-style jeeps roaring across the field were hard to get. I ignored them, as I ignored the individual soldiers scattered across the terrain. In the heat of battle, all enemy fire on our position was ignored. I had enough to aim for already. The handwheel in my left hand. The trigger guard in my right. The strap rattled through the hands of the Alsatian, cartridge by cartridge. His open hands looked as if they were spread out in prayer. The smoke spreading around the cooling jacket indicated the overheating of the barrel. So, opening the barrel change flap. Barrel out. Replacement barrel in. *Brrr, Brrr, Brrr.* "Hans, we're low on ammo!" I ignored the urgent call of my comrade. The columns just kept coming. Their tips were already dipping behind the edge of the terrain and were soon out of my range. Every Russian I caught today I did not have to face tomorrow. Logic was so plain during the war.

    A loud puffing in the background told me that our gunners 3 and 4 had relentlessly supplied ammunition to our position. The backpack had been empty for a long time by now and lay redundant on the slippery, cold farmland. The constant visual strain clouded my brain. The targets began to blur into each other. My aim was no longer precise. "Gunner change, fast!" I stooped to the left. Ankle-deep in brass and empty cartridge belts entangled in a huge Gordian knot, while the Alsatian clamped the MG. We were soon running out of ammunition again. One of the two young Jäger noticed that too and jumped into the field drainage without even batting an eyelid, off for supplies once again. Like an oiled bolt, ignoring the shrapnel whizzing about him, he rushed to the edge of the village. The water in the ditch splashed wildly to all sides. About halfway there, an invisible punch threw him to one side. He lay limply on the edge of the ditch. The second ammunition runner, another young Jäger, wanted to jump after him. I pulled him back down by his camouflage jacket. "Stay, I'll go!" I put the rucksack on and started crawling through the drainage. My arms soon sank up to their elbows into the brown water. My boots, pants, and outerwear were soaking wet. I passed the crippled feet of the comrade. I immediately saw that he was dead. Fountains of blood gushed from his neck onto his camouflage jacket. His broken eyes were still turned to the edge of the village. The last goal of his self-sacrificed young life. I arrived at the company headquarters totally out of breath and collided with a signal man storming out of the door.

"We need MG ammo!"

"It's all gone, you have to go to the church."

Up above the rooftops, the striking spire showed the way. I had already noticed it when we arrived three days ago, when we had marched to the main square not far from the church to relieve the Panzergrenadiers. The weight of my drenched clothes made running difficult, but I kept going. Heavily laden Jäger were coming toward me. Covered in layer after layer of MG ammo belts, they looked like Christmas trees. I spotted a truck parked close to the church wall. Ammunition was issued to the surrounding Landser directly from the open truck bed. I held my mountain rucksack out to the soldier frantically handing out supplies. He tore open some of the ammo boxes and emptied their contents into the rucksack until it was full to the brim. I quickly hung another two cartridge belts round my neck and grabbed an ammo box with each hand.

I stormed back to where I was needed with undiminished

haste. I suddenly seemed to fly. My feet gently lifted off the floor. A glaring light hit me. Then I smashed into something hard, almost crushing my lungs. Lying on my side, I studied the wild zigzag pattern of the cobblestones. I could see soldiers lying on it, seemingly asleep. A hellish pain exploded in my left side. A tear ran diagonally across my nose and fell to the floor. And then I saw a pair of mountain boots right beside me. A figure stooped down to me. I wanted to scream for help, but I could only mumble. The figure pulled the MG straps from my neck and disappeared from view. My eyes slowly shut. Finished ...

CHAPTER 8

THE END IS NIGH

The attack had finally succeeded. The Soviets had no choice but to flee. Not before they'd wiped out a German grenadier company blocking the way, though. The following losses reported by 3 GD testify to the severity of the battle: 852 dead enemies counted. 14 tanks destroyed, 6 of them in close combat. More than 100 anti-tank guns, field guns, and mortars captured or destroyed. Lots of wagons, trucks, and other military equipment. 34 prisoners is an almost negligible amount given all the rest. It had long since gone out of fashion with the Soviets to be captured. In their fight for their beloved "Mother Russia," they rather died a heroic death. The same thing was true for us, except that the additional specter "Siberia" strengthened our sense of duty.

The result of the successful tank battle in the Puszta satisfied the German generals for only a short period of time. The plan had worked. Considerable parts of the surrounded cavalry escaped, but lost all equipment. It would take them several weeks to get back to full operational strength. In addition to that, some of the important traffic junctions had fallen back into German hands. Nyíregyháza and, further north, Tokaj, to name just two. All this enabled the orderly retreat of the German 8th Army from behind the Tisza. As painful as the defeat at Nyíregyháza may have been for the enemy, this tactical victory did not exactly turn the tables. On the contrary. While all of this was going on, the Soviet High Command had assembled its 2nd Ukrainian Front. This time between the Drava and the Lower Tisza. With a size equivalent to one of the German Army Groups. The four strong corps entered Budapest on October 29. The Wehrmacht and Waffen-SS units available resisted in vain. They were swept aside by the armored and infantry masses of the Red Army. In the face of the Red superiority, some Hungarian units vacated their positions or ran over to the enemy. In the opinion of the German High Command, the possibility of a second tank battle was completely out of the question. Their panzer divisions had been fighting at Debrecen and Nyíregyháza for over a month now and were completely burned out. Or as it is called in military jargon, "not suitable for further attacks." 3 GD had also been severely affected by the fighting in the Puszta. The number of dead, wounded, and missing comrades was in the hundreds. The constant loss of experienced officers, senior Jäger, and whole weapon teams was particularly painful. The brunt of the fight had rested on their shoulders during those many battles. They alone had learned how to cope with dangerous situations. The replacements assigned from home could fill the ranks of the divisions in number only. The short training was far from sufficient to resist the war-tested opponent. Let alone to get used to the front. It took a while to learn how to survive. Just as it had been the case with me in Nikopol. Where replacement crews arrived, they were immediately thrown into the fray. With the bitter result that they filled their homes' obituaries.

When I opened my eyes, I found myself in a ghostly gloom.

It smelled of mold and iodine. I lay flat on a spartanly stiff pad. My pupils dilated to let in more light. To my right, a yellowish glow began to appear out of the darkness. As I turned my head slightly in its direction, I immediately felt a burning pain in my cervical region. But there was something over there—a stretched linen cloth. Covered in large dark patches. In the pale candlelight I could see human figures moving behind it. Someone seemed to be working on something with rhythmic movements. In their hand, an object that looked like a bow saw. I heard a gnarly moan. I knew the sound a saw made when applied to flesh. I had heard it time and time again back home on the farm, when my father skillfully dissected a freshly slaughtered pig. The hair on the back of my neck stood up. Goosebumps spread over my body like wildfire. But there was no feeling on my left side. I put my hand down past my hips to my thigh. My heart started beating faster and faster. I felt rough linen firmly wrapped around my leg, held in place by metal clips. I did not get any further. My abdominal muscles failed to comply. My God—was my leg gone? Heart and lungs rocked each other in ever more violent thrusts. They almost seemed to burst under my soul's despair. Crippled, at nineteen years? What would become of me? My chest quivered feverishly. And once again the emotional shock intensified, only to turn into a confused mental game of life and death. I finally closed my eyes and lost consciousness once again.

It had been around lunchtime. The brave Jäger battalions had relentlessly pushed toward the outskirts of Nyíregyháza. The close combat with the Russian Guardsmen had gotten wilder and wilder. Our artillery fired at the detected enemy anti-tank guns with clockwork precision. From the western edge of the city, German "Panther" tanks and grenadiers mounted on armored personnel carriers were already pushing toward the center. Speeding through the streets, they had split the enemy into smaller groups. The trailing infantry then took house after house and broke the last resistance. The Russian military command post south of Nagykálló received increasingly desperate transmissions from the divisions involved. In a correct assessment of the hopeless situation, the Russian general in charge of the operation gave the order to break out toward the southeast. Likewise, he released the last reserves of artillery ammunition to support the outbreak. So, as I was heading back with my rucksack swinging on my shoulder, I heard the first shots. They sounded like they were many kilometers away. Rocket launchers, the Katyushas, were sending their deadly rocket cargo up to the sky. Not even thirty seconds later, the first wave hit the churchyard. Dozens of missile projectiles detonated almost simultaneously on the hard cobblestones. Their splinters ate mercilessly into the Jäger rushing to the ammunition truck. The soldier handing out supplies fell headfirst from the loading dock. He was fatally wounded. Two signal men rushing over the church square disappeared in a cloud of fire and iron. All comrades waiting at the truck were either killed or wounded. The blast of the nearby explosion lifted me up in the air and slammed me against the church wall. At the same time, fingernail-sized metal shrapnel drilled into my left leg. From the ankle right up to the hip, pulling rags of the soaking wet field trousers and long johns with it.

As the smoke cleared, a small squad of Jäger came running to grab ammunition for their hard-pressed comrades. They could not take care of the soldiers lying in the middle of a churchyard-turned-graveyard, but instead collected all the ammunition that was lying around. Only a brave Hungarian who had watched the disaster from his basement window ran out to rescue me. He carried my limp body over his strong shoulders to the nearest dressing station. A wide set of basement stairs led down to an empty wine cellar. The arched basement segments had been converted into makeshift beds. The plaster was peeling from the damp walls. The whole ceiling was covered in black mold. In the farthest corner, an improvised operating theater. Separated from the rest of the basement room by only a sloppily stretched linen sheet. There, the senior physician and his three paramedics did everything humanly possible to avert imminent disasters. They operated, cleaned, and sutured the whole night. Hopelessly lacerated limbs fell victim to the bone saw. They landed in a tin tub stinking of blood and cold meat.

Methodically, the gravely wounded were separated from the lightly injured. Because of my severely bleeding wounds, I was seen quite quickly. As I lay in the pool of blood of the Jäger they had operated on previously, my foot was hurriedly tied off far above the knee. With this, the little blood rivulets coming from a dozen or so fleshy openings finally dried up. When the senior physician realized I had no life-threatening wounds, he let them bed me down on an old door panel. A paramedic knelt beside me, and in the glaring light of a field lantern he began to pull the pieces of metal and the scraps of cloth out of my skin. He must have been experienced. He cleaned and disinfected every cut and wound with German thoroughness. He pulled out all foreign objects with tweezers and wiped them off on his blood-colored apron. He then closed the gaps in my skin with a few stitches. He wrapped the leg in a thick cloth bandage, gave me a tetanus shot, and covered me with a warm blanket. It helped that I was completely unconscious during the entire process. The paramedic was able to do his work in peace. And, in all my misfortune, I had been extremely lucky.

I woke up the next day in the overflowing wine cellar. The comrades around me suffered in silence. The senior physician sunken into a wooden chair. His peacefully sleeping countenance made the slaughterhouse seem somewhat grotesque. A rumbling coming from the stairs announced the arrival of more trouble. Two Landser carried a seriously wounded man. It was a young boy of no more than eighteen years old. The senior physician was immediately back on his feet, wiping the sleep from his eyes and putting his glasses back on his nose. He gestured in the direction of the dirty linen cloth. Then he set to work. I do not remember how long I lay in that stinking damp basement. The impressions, however, burned themselves deep into my memory. The terrible, sad pictures provided material for lifelong soul-searching nightmares. The smell of cold, carelessly disposed-of human flesh in a tin bath remains unforgettable. It could not get any worse. It was hell on earth. Created by a human hand which had set out to create a new paradise. Whether it had been driven by one political motive or the other, in the end, nothing had changed.

At a certain point, they stretchered me out. Thick rain dripped onto my face. The weather was still miserable. The temperatures were just above zero and the rain was continuous. I sucked the fresh winter air greedily into my lungs, letting it replace the cellar's musty odor. Next, they crammed us into a medical truck and drove us to the heavily battered train station. There was just one locomotive. Already blowing steam. We were loaded into the empty carriages. Skeptical as always, I perceived that the outer walls were spared from any red cross markings. "This will be fun," I thought, hoping the cloud cover would last for the duration of the trip. Otherwise, we'd be a snack presented on a silver platter for the Russian strafers. My head was still slightly ringing from the concussion. Although I could hardly move my left leg because of the thick bandage, I felt the constant pumping of my body's self-healing powers. The train began to move without giving a signal. Were we going home? I hoped so, though no one could provide reliable information. After not even three hours we suddenly stopped. When the carriage door slid open, I saw "Miskolc" written on the platform in big letters. That did not sound like home at all.

"Come on, comrades, this is it. The locomotive has to return to Nyíregyháza immediately and load the heavy weapons. We're just retreating to behind the Tisza."

These words of the military policeman did not go down well. They were followed by restrained curses about the war and about the authorities. A Gebirgsjäger who had been paralyzed from the waist down mentioned Hitler's name in the same breath as that of the crazy Emperor Nero. Our belief in the supreme leadership was shaken to the core. So far they had only brought us misery and suffering. The military policeman could hardly ignore the remarks, but what should he do? Send us to a penal battalion? Or maybe report us to the senior officer responsible? In spite of the pronounced severity of the German security services at that time, there were more urgent matters than putting straight a handful of wounded soldiers.

We finally ended up in a real hospital. There were hospital beds with white sheets and heavenly soft feather pillows. The peace there was not only a treat for the body but also for the soul. German nurses were busily caring for the Landser that had been saved from death's door. Our bandages were changed daily, and we also received hot meals on a daily basis. In between, I went in for check-ups. The X-ray showed that a fragment of shrapnel of about one centimeter had been left behind. It was situated just below the ankle joint. And, oddly enough, it was precisely this place that did not hurt at all. So the doctors decided not to carry out what may have been a difficult operation. "It will probably grow out one day. It's nothing dramatic." Those were the casual words of the duty doctor. Compared to other comrades, I had certainly had a lucky escape. Amputations, complete blindness, severe facial deformations—the hospital was a panopticon of disfigured human bodies. Some were so severely wounded that they were completely dependent. I was also dependent on the nurses when it came to daily body care. Lying on my back or turned slightly to the side, a twenty-year-old woman scrubbed the dirt from my skin. After a while, a thick, foaming layer of mud had formed on the water's surface in the bucket. She drove the washcloth over my back and arms and between my legs briskly. The only caution the nurse ever exercised was when she got to the bandaged area. I was deeply embarrassed. My previous encounters with the opposite sex had been at school or at the village fete and had been limited to exchanging stealthy glances. I had never kissed a girl, although I had been particularly interested in the daughter of a neighboring farmer. But the war had put an end to that. These women provided laborious, selfless service. They tried to distract us from the dark shadow of the war with songs and card games and often enough they also had fathers, husbands, or brothers fighting for their skins on some distant patch of the earth.

The visits of the hospital staff offered the only distraction. There was not much to do with the other wounded alone. Close to me lay a tank soldier from East Prussia. While fighting in the Puszta he had suffered a hideous abdominal injury. The second he was about to leave his burning tank some pieces of shrapnel hit him and, just his luck, they literally cut off his testicles. He had just taken his fiancée as a bride on his last visit home. Now he had to deal with the certainty that he would never be able to start a family. Most of our discussions remained taciturn. And it was not much better on the other side of the bed either. The face of the Landser lying there had swollen to a thick balloon. A bullet had passed through both cheeks, tearing his tongue to pieces. All he could bring out was a loud howl. I used the time and made note of my impressions in my pocket diary. In between, I wrote a long letter home which I concluded with the calming, almost self-therapeutic words: "Apart from this I am doing well, and we will certainly see each other again soon."

It soon became apparent that Miskolc was by no means safe. The worn-out remnants of the German 8th Army, pursued by the advancing divisions of the Red Army, had withdrawn to behind the Tisza at the beginning of November. Wehrmacht units were already flowing through the industrial city on the eastern edge of the Bükk Mountains. The two Jäger regiments of 3 GD held their positions close to the gates of the city. As of mid-November, no fewer than six enemy rifle divisions, one cavalry division, and two mechanized brigades were forcing their way toward them. The enemy outnumbered them at least seven to one! When it came to their number of guns, tanks, and aircraft, the ratio looked even less favorable for the Wehrmacht. Surely there could be no talk of another turnaround. Fighting on meant a rather desperate delay of the ever-approaching defeat.

When the eviction order for the hospital finally arrived, we were severely underequipped. Transport space was limited, and the trucks had to struggle over the ground made soggy by the constant rain or clogged up by Hungarian refugees. In other words, the roads were bad, and progress slow. The well-developed railway line to Budapest was already occupied in several places, so no wounded could be deported there. The northbound railway line was in a similar condition. It led into Slovak territory, an area whose population was basically considered an ally of the German Reich. After the Slovak national uprising between September and October 1944, however, the territory was increasingly haunted by partisans. They blew up bridges, railways, and telegraph poles in nightly attacks and even took on German security posts. Forward, backward, and to the side—a conflagration of almost apocalyptic proportions raged on all sides.

So the hospital slowly emptied. The heavily wounded were transported away with a heavy heart. What remained were those who would soon see recovery even without any special care. And that included me. One day, a well-fed officer in a long black leather coat entered the infirmary. The front row of the buttons of his coat tightened under the pressure of his enormous gut. He must have lived well in this neck of the woods, I thought to myself. A few feet behind him were armed military police with submachine guns. My expression darkened. I suspected bad news heading my way. Especially since I had already heard the rumors about this lot. They were volunteering personnel, which we called "General Heldenklau." After the start of the Russian campaign and the resulting high number of casualties in the Wehrmacht, there was a need to open the door to new manpower resources. This included rear services, supplies, and field hospitals. This officer strode through the long rows of beds with his arms crossed behind his back and asked the attending physician to explain the findings. After a brief assessment he gave instructions to the sergeant behind him, who scribbled them zealously down in his notebook. The closer he came, the clearer became his words.

"Oh, just a bagatelle then—is to report to Emergency Company A by the afternoon. Foot injuries? Well, the unit is fully motorized. Trained radio operator? We need him! He will be assigned to my staff ..."

That's how it went. All the objections of the chief physician were brushed aside by the arrogant slogans of this jackass. After all, it was all about the Endsieg here. The decisive battle in the east. And here in this hospital, there were still enough suitable souls who would be able to make a contribution. One thing was clear to me: I did not want to end up in an emergency company or improvised battle group. Even by the standards of the eastern war, the survival prospects in such units were well below zero. By now my bandage had been replaced by plaster casts, and the past few days I had been able to walk about a bit. This left me with no illusions about my fate. Therefore, I decided to make the best of the situation and go on the offensive. And before fatty even arrived at my bed, I received him with the following words:

"Lieutenant Colonel, sir, good to see you, sir! I have been wanting to return to my unit. I have been considering myself operational for the past few days. My regiment is right outside town. You couldn't help me with that by any chance, could you?"

Perplexed by my youthful impudence, he raised his eyebrows and looked at the medical officer, who only shrugged and waved his hand.

"Which Regiment?"

"Gebirgsjäger 138, sir!"

"Well then get a discharge permit and contact your unit by nightfall at the latest." He leaned across to the field police. "Record name, rank, and unit, and get a report from his sergeant major in the morning."

This ended my hospital stay as abruptly as it had begun. Being sent home for recovery had never been on the table anyway. At least I managed to go back to my MG gang. Nearly three and a half weeks had passed since I'd been injured. The short break had still done wonders for my body and my mind. I had regained weight and had been able to rest extensively. Catching one last breath before the final act of the war. From now on, the spiral of death would move faster and faster. Crushing and devouring all life. To be honest, I had hardly any hopes to come out of this alive. But at least I had learned how to sell my life dearly by now.

I made my way back to the front on the back of a "Kettenkrad" (a half-tracked vehicle with a motorbike-like front). These were normally used to take supplies to the front. After not even four hours I had already reached my unit. That's how close our positions were. At the company headquarters they received me with much relief. I had known the duty sergeant since Romania. I had been considered missing since the battle over Nagykálló, thanks to our terrible reporting system. I got new field trousers, marching equipment, and a semi-automatic carbine from the stores. I shuddered when I realized that the carbine still had the previous owner's blood stuck to it. I hastily wiped it off with the elbow pad of my camouflage jacket. Then I joined the food line, which was just about to be dished out rations, and I finally met my comrades just before midnight. The Alsatian fell around my neck without saying a word. The still-aching leg and the terrible impressions of the musty cellar hole were suddenly forgotten. It was strange. Nowhere did I feel more at home than with this gang. Everything seemed so familiar. Even the two or three new faces who had replaced the fallen. After a few days of fighting, they would be dearer to me than any friend from before the war.

We stayed in our positions only a few days. Snow and rain worked in shifts. There was ankle-high water everywhere. In the morning it was sometimes covered with a layer of thin ice. We were frozen to the bone. Building a fire was unthinkable because the Russians were in our immediate vicinity. And to top it all off, it was sniper high season again.

During the hubbub called retreat, we finally received our marching order. Miskolc had become untenable. Russian troops had broken through at various other spots of the front. Here we go again. One night, as we were clearing the trenches, an enemy propaganda speaker echoed to us:

"German soldier, give yourself up. You are fighting for a lost cause ..."

Well, we knew that. But surrender? After all the sacrifice?

"German soldier. Surrender to the Red Army now, we will look after you well."

From a long line of marching Jäger, one of us suddenly spoke out loud into the silent winter night:

"Shut the fuck up, Ivan!"

Exactly what we were all thinking. For just a moment, this brought a smile to my face.

The division managed to successfully break away from the enemy and formed something like a coherent front at the height of the Slovak Ore Mountains. Once again, we entered a mountainous, wooded terrain, more suitable for a mountain troop. No one even waisted a thought on the Hungarian lowland. It had only brought us misfortune. The losses during the grueling battles for Nyíregyháza and Miskolc had torn holes that could no longer be mended. The harsh winter made life difficult, but at the same time it also made it difficult for the enemy to reroute. The sustained defensive battles lasted until the turn of the year.

My comrades and I were often right in the thick of things. Unfortunately, I still had problems with my left leg. Especially on those strenuous marches. The larger wounds tore open and began to inflame. Even our sergeant saw that no war was to be won with a limping soldier. Without further ado, he assigned me a job with the company squad where I was supposed to recover completely.

So I was handed a packhorse with a small cart. I had been used to working with animals ever since I was a child, and I set up a seat on the two-axle carriage from which I could direct the horse. I named it "Nesta II" in memory of my father's faithful draft horse. After just a few days, we were welded into an inseparable team. Nesta II tirelessly progressed and overcame even the steepest climbs. Needless to say, after completing the replenishment orders, I did not rest until I had fed the horse and freed him from the chafing straps. The mutual support created trust between the human and the animal, despite the inhospitable conditions. I nearly lost her once. I was on a supply tour just behind the main front line when I was surprised by a swelling howl. These were volleys of Katyusha rocket launchers which I knew only too well. I jumped into a cowshed and threw myself into the corner. A split second later, the missiles hit the surrounding buildings. Splinters hissed through the wooden stable and bored into the mud wall opposite. The shelling was over as quick as it had started. My first concern was my horse, of course. I stepped outside with very little hope and saw only the overturned cart lying on the ground. Saddened and emptyhanded, I made my way back to the company headquarters. After a few hundred meters, I suddenly heard a loud whinny. Miraculously, Nesta II seeking salvation in flight had caught his bridle in the undergrowth. The animal stood there trembling all over and was certainly as happy as I was to have company again.

The supply task allowed me to keep in contact with the other units too, and I got a lot of information first-hand. The dominant theme these days was the constant threat of partisans. At a place higher up, one even spoke of "pest-like conditions" which seemed to increase day by day. The Slovak popular uprising had been broken by German security forces in such a brutal way that the mood of the local population was not amenable to say the least. No wonder, after the indiscriminate mass shootings and abominable crimes against the civilian population. Among the units deployed was, for example, the SS special unit "Dirlewanger," named after the Waffen-SS General, Oskar Dirlewanger. It consisted largely of former inmates of concentration camps and detention centers and had acquired a dubious reputation, not only in the partisan battles in Belarus, but also later on in the suppression of the Warsaw Uprising.

In the thirties, Dirlewanger himself had served time for the rape of a minor but was later pardoned because of his good connections with senior Nazi officials. The sadistic actions of these and other units involved in the suppression of the Slovak National Uprising had produced exactly the opposite of what was actually in the interest of the fighting front soldier: pacification of the hinterland and thus secure access to supplies. The aftermath of this partisan fight, free from all common rules of war, was now felt by 3 GD. The indigenous population was filled with deep anger and hatred toward everything German. I could see it in their eyes. Young or old, everyone seemed to be conspiring against us. In contrast to the Hungarians, no support was to be expected from the Slovaks. Even shelter in this snow-covered country had to be obtained by force. It was clear to everyone from the simple Landser to the unit leader that there would be retaliations in the form of assassinations. There was little we could do about it, however. And so, the day before Christmas Eve, situated at the end of the supply line, I trudged straight into an ambush.

The first shots pelted out of nowhere and immediately claimed casualties. The terrain was disorienting. A narrow, looping valley road flanked by steep slopes. There was no sign of anything but snow and forest. So I tried desperately to turn the cart around and get behind the next bend. An accompanying Jäger squad had thrown themselves into the ditch and started a firefight to allow the rest of the column to get into position. A hopeless venture. Confused soldiers fled backward, closely followed by a group of stray horses scattering their load during their panicked gallop or having it all hanging unnaturally on their flanks. Just as I was about to cross the road, Nesta II received a heavy blow to one of her flanks. My faithful companion fell to the ground like a stone and remained motionless. MG salvos drove through the thin planking of the wagon. I did not hesitate for a second and jumped headlong into the nearby ditch. Pressed tightly to the ground, I crawled and reached the lifesaving bend after about 50 meters. From there, together with several other trembling Landser, I followed the diminishing battle of the Jäger squad. Hardly anyone had taken his weapon in their chaotic flight. When hand grenade explosions came up close, there was no time to stop. Everyone stormed back to where we had come from. At some point we ran straight into a Jäger company that was about to start a counterattack. I recognized their leader from a previous supply tour.

Without even looking at us, this gang unfolded into the densely forested mountain slopes to quickly save what was left to save. The battle noise was extinct by now. So I joined the Jäger hanging back on the road and charged forward with them.

But it was too late. The column had been almost completely wiped out. Horse carcasses lay strewn beside fallen Landser. In between some wrecked carriages, some of them still burning. My cart at the end of the column had only been lightly damaged by the bombardment. Cold comfort. The partisans had done a great job. They had silently been submerged by the white nothing. Long before the attacking spearhead of the Jäger company had even approached. Nesta II was still laying in the cold slippery slush. In the same spot where she had been hit. Bloody foam gurgled from her mouth. Her whole body shook under the pain of the torn organs. A terrible picture that would have upset me no less if the horse had been a human. I could not stand the sight of the loyal horse suffering, so I took the semiautomatic from the cart and chased a bullet through her frontal bone. With a last gasp she finally found peace. I kneeled beside my four-legged comrade and closed her eyes in a last human gesture.

"There. Someone is still alive there! Quick, stretcher, over there!" The new task wiped away my grief in seconds. But what remained was deep bitterness and the longing for speedy revenge. The incidental guerrilla attack marked the end of a creeping development that had begun shortly after I had left home. I had become completely engrossed in the war. My whole state of mind was geared to it. As contemptible as this may seem in hindsight, from now on peace only existed in death. My mind and those of my still-fighting comrades were basically mirror images of the apocalypse around us. No one could permanently shut out the countless traumatic experiences that were on the agenda at the time. The souls of the men became increasingly raw. Unstoppable.

Just before the turn of the year, I met my school friend Toni. While moving further backward, the path of our two regiments happened to cross once again. This time at a large fork in the road. At our last meeting, during the retreat in Ukraine, he had sported that mischievous grin that I knew from our youth. That youth had come to an abrupt end when we'd donned the uniform. In December 1944, barely a year later, the grin had gone. Toni had aged at least ten years in the meantime. His ice-blue eyes sat deep in their black-shaded caves. The sniper rifle dangled from his chest. Our brief exchange was completely emotionless. I told him about my injury two months ago and the deceitful attack of the partisans. But he almost did not hear what I said. All he kept talking about was having to repay the Russians in kind. He seemed to be carrying a heavy emotional burden. I relied on my gut feeling and did not dig deeper. After a brief handshake and an attempt at a contrite smile, he rejoined the slow-moving column. Secretly watching him go, I started pondering. I grabbed a passing Jäger by the sleeve and pulled him out of the line.

"Tell me, what's the matter with Toni?"

"Oh him, yes, since Miskolc he's been completely done in. Thinks he has the death of a little Hungarian girl on his conscience. A Russian sniper had been after him but caught the girl instead. Headshot. She was trying to bring him a jug of milk. Now he is constantly on the prowl. Doesn't sleep anymore. Has gone through three spotters in the last four weeks. Nobody wants to go out with him anymore. Comrade, I have to carry on."

"Yes. Thanks."

The nameless Landser's story did not leave me untouched. At least it was plausible and lifted the veil of uncertainty. Every frontline soldier had to carry his load. Some a little, some a lot. This included many things that were never talked about. For example, if you had the death of a comrade on your conscience—something that happened all too often in the chaos of battle. Or if your own brutality got out of hand in the bloody onslaught and burned its cruel impressions into your soul for all eternity. Nobody was immune to it. Nobody could escape this burden. Not even the toughest soldiers. After the loss of Nesta II, I immediately returned to my platoon. The mood of the comrades, who had already been depressed, had slumped even further. In the meantime, the Alsatian's home had become a battle zone. His last attempted contact with his loved ones had remained unanswered. He was consumed with worry.

But the long arm of the war had done much worse to our sergeant. One day, after our mail had been handed out, he collapsed into a howling heap. What had happened to him shook even the most hardened Jäger to the core. After the devastating bombing of downtown Graz on November 1, 1944, his wife and three small children had miserably suffocated in an air raid shelter. A stroke of fate that cannot be put into words. Only a few weeks earlier they had left their home close to the Hungarian border to avoid the approaching Red Army. They had found shelter with relatives in Graz. A veteran Oberjäger was forced to take command. The sergeant was practically unreachable for several days. He met the approaching field chaplain with the words:

"Where was your god when my family needed him? I do not need him anymore now!"

Yet after the first major battle he was back in charge. With an eerie longing for death. He seemed to be looking for every last bullet. Oddly enough he always got away, no matter how bad the cards were stacked. It seemed as if the God he had denied did not want to let him die. As if He still had a task in mind for him.

The Christmas holiday could not uplift the miserable mood. On the contrary. On December 24, there was a lot of harassing fire all through the night. On December 25, we secured a reconnaissance troop that had suffered so many casualties shortly after the start of their mission that the whole thing was canceled on the spot. On December 26, there was a break-in in the neighboring positions, where the Russians took two prisoners and slaughtered the rest of the crew down to the last man. All of this was very different from the romantically transfigured Christmas front reports from the First World War. I could only bitterly turn up my nose. A resourceful Landser who on Christmas Eve conjured up a Christmas tree with improvised decorations? Last-minute gift packages from home? A suppressed but joyous "Silent Night" in a safe shelter? The dreary reality of the 1944 wartime Christmas could hardly have been further removed from such a festival of love, peace, and unity.

The new year did not change the situation. It greeted us with a raging fireworks display. Not from the German pipes, because the ammunition was already far too scarce, but from the opposite side. As a result of the early-morning attack, the Russians were now sitting on a commanding ridge in the back of our regiment. We were not told much more than that, when our MG platoon, a group twenty men strong, was assigned to the counterattack. The Jäger companies were already so bled out, that different smaller groups of the battalion staff and some of the regimental staff were added. I recognized some faces from my short time on light duty. The supporting weapons, mainly MGs and grenade launchers, should be equipped with a minimum of personnel to maximize the infantry force. So I finally found myself in one of the two attacking groups of eighty men each. The time for attack had been set at noon. That was due to the time it took to bring the widely scattered groups of reserves over the snowy winter trails. The group I belonged to was to attack from the front while the other was to attack the right flank. We moved into our positions midmorning and waited. After hours of nervous waiting, the redeeming signal finally came. Following this, the officers and NCOs threw their fists into the air three times. With a jerk and with frozen limbs, the leached-out pile rose from the undergrowth. A fear-driven run down a slight dip and then 200 meters up the slope. Not a single shot from the opposite side. It was only our MGs and grenade launchers that broke the silence. Panting away, I tried to keep up with the sergeant. He had almost reached the upper edge of the terrain while most of the Jäger were still passing through the depression. And there, a hand-grenade blast. Barking MP salvos. Russian commands. I arrived at the top even before the enemy had gathered. Jumped hard to the left into a ditch and knocked down a heavily staggering Red Army soldier with my rifle butt. On we went to a semi-finished shelter in which the stove was still glowing, and it was stinking of alcohol fumes. Loud cries from the adjacent edge of the forest told me that our flanking thrust was in full swing.

The surprise attack was a success. But not, as it turned out later, through any German fighting skill, but through the utter innocuousness of the Russians. They had doused their previous success and the New Year with vodka. Scarcely any of the soldiers running headfirst into the German flank were sober. Some were so drunk they were still lying on their straw sacks in some of the surrounding huts. They had to be roused by several kicks until they finally regained their senses.

The counterattack had been successful, much to our relief. As a further result, we had sustained only a handful of slightly wounded Jäger, but we got our hands on rich spoils and well over a hundred prisoners. It was to be the last of my successes during the course of the war. At least of that scale. That night, my gang was sent out and used for defense tasks elsewhere. In the brief moments I had to sleep between guard shifts, I was plagued by nightmarish fantasies. I jumped each time a comrade grabbed me by the shoulder asking to be relieved of his duty. The next day we learned that after heavy artillery fire, the enemy had taken the hill for a second time. Shortly after, we were gathered again to fix the situation. This time, mainly due to the lack of surprise and a now-sober opponent, we had to accept the circumstances and press on, come what may. We were already under heavy fire when we stormed into the valley. The comrade to my left was dropped by MG fire.

This surprise assault ended bitterly with the first casualties. We worked our way forward in individual leaps. The Alsatian had positioned himself in the hollow and kept firing at the Russian muzzle flashes. Shortly before we got to the first huts, we were under such intense fire that we could almost not leave the place. My instinct of self-preservation was activated by the balls of fire hissing over me and prevented me from getting up. Any jump forward would have been my last. When I looked right and left, I realized that not too many of my comrades had come through. I dug myself into the snow-covered ground as best I could. Charging forward or retreating had become impossible under these circumstances. Hot blood shot to my head. The feeling of panic was soon followed by a blunt feeling of indifference. The redeeming thrust finally came from the second group backing us up. They managed to break into the Russian positions and fight them down after a hard struggle. The result was shocking. Almost half of the men who had attacked with me were either dead or wounded. The calls for medics echoed across the battlefield. The long pools of blood gave the snow-white slope a macabre countenance. Some of the wounded hobbled back to the starting position, supported by comrades. Fortunately, both the Alsatian and the sergeant were still physically intact. We had been victorious, but at what price? A few days later, the insignificant hill had to be cleared anyway as we moved north across the town of Žilina. What's more, the supreme war strategists of the German Wehrmacht saw Slovakia and the Czech heartland behind it as only a secondary battlefield. The main show was on elsewhere—in the west, in the Ardennes to be precise, where a last desperate offensive against the Americans was underway; to the east on the Vistula where the Russian armies had torn everything to the ground. Budapest had been surrounded since Christmas. The Balkans were already lost. In Italy the Allies had once again gone on the offensive, seeking to push through the Alps. In short, there were fires raging all around. A military turning point? Hopeless! The enemy hordes were bigger than ever. The closer we got back to the German Reich, the grimmer the confrontations became. Our losses steadily increased in the firestorm infernos. Battalions melted into companies and companies to platoons. During the arduous march back through the Váh basin, 3 GD on the situation maps of the Wehrmacht command staff was now only classified as a battle group. Just like its neighboring divisions, it was a shadow of its former self. But in the High Tatras and the Beskids, the division was still able to hold its own for some time. Despite all the signs of decline. Despite the lack of heavy weapons. Despite the inferior cartridge cases, which brought us many a calamitous MG jam. The Wehrmacht was bleeding from countless wounds.

By the end of March, we happened to pass a field post office that was about to close. Taking the opportunity, I put my pocket diary along with a few sloppily scribbled lines in an envelope and addressed it to my parents. If fate were to catch up with me, at least something of mine would remain. Notes from my front experiences, names of dear comrades, and a few nice words to the family. What else should a nineteen-year-old MG gunner in the middle section of the Eastern Front expect? It was clear to everyone that the final act was imminent, that defeat was inevitable, and it was only a matter of time. Among my lot, no one talked about a final victory anymore. The much-praised miracle weapons had turned out to be empty words of far-away propaganda magistrates. Even the fanatical party supporters had become subdued in the meantime.

Nonetheless, it was clear that we would empty the goblet of want and death together until the very end. It was an unspoken, blood-signed pact of men who were forged together in the furnace of war. We felt and acted that way even on the eve of defeat.

This eve had seen the last major withdrawal movement of the division towards the saving west. Orders were issued by the Army Group and so the XLIX Gebirgsjäger Corps and 3 GD suddenly stood still. Holding back for the protection of the Moravian Ostrava industrial area. After Nikopol and the Szekler Zipfel, this was the third time in almost two years that the division occupied the easternmost point of the Eastern

Front. A dangerously exposed position that was about to be taken from the north and south. By the end of April, Bratislava, Vienna, and Brno had already fallen. Russian tank spearheads were also pushing sharply toward Dresden and Prague. In Berlin, the final decisive battle raged. What the simple Landser could not have known but the German High Command knew very well was that the clock had already struck five past twelve, as far as withdrawal was concerned.

With a stony face and downcast eyes, the sergeant had walked up before the assembled platoon. We stood in a semicircle in a small forest near Frýdek. The platoon that was maybe three or four MG crews and a few riflemen. Monotonously, he rattled off the just-obtained company commands and the most up-to-date status of the war at large. There were words such as "soon to be surrounded," "gap between Olomouc and Brno," and "rearguard mission." When he said that word, he suddenly looked up. He would lead that one himself and only take two volunteers. One MG squad. The rest would join the company to head west as fast as possible. Suddenly I felt in my stomach that dull feeling that you usually have when running behind schedule. One hopes to be able to make up for the delay but secretly knows that the last train has long departed.

"Who is coming with me?"

Nearly all of used raised our hand. Almost reflexively. The Alsatian and I did it at the same time without so much as glancing at each other first.

"No family men. And no freshers." And then, after a short pause: "Kahr and Waeber. Get yourself ready. The rest is to report to Sergeant Hollerer."

It was clear what was to be done in these last few days. A final suicide mission. I was fully aware of that. Home was within reach. That weighed on me heavily. Maybe 200 kilometers away. At least to the border, which was rumored to already be occupied by the Russians. As always, such thoughts were wiped away during the bustle which initiated every departure.

We picked up some more ammo and food supplies, and our little troop disappeared into the woods. The sergeant walked some ways ahead. Behind him was the Alsatian with the machine gun, and I was close behind with the tripod mount on my back. This was the strategy: if we came across the enemy or some Czech partisans, they would almost certainly catch the front man. The followers, that is to say the Alsatian and I, would then be warned to beat it. Our little three-man squad was far too weak for a serious confrontation anyway.

Just before dusk we were huddled close together on some nameless fork. In a so-called shielding position, to allow the undisturbed retreat of our comrades. Throughout the night I heard engines roar and horses neigh. Heavily packed columns driven by only one goal: to avoid Russian captivity. Come what may! The noise slowly disappeared into the distance, and by the early hours of the morning, there was a deadly silence. That was the sign for us to pack up and sneak back toward the west, avoiding paths as much as possible. That went on for days. Sometimes we met our own troops, sometimes we saw not a soul for quite some time. The emotional burden was great. The idea to stay behind omnipresent. Strangely, the enemy was in no hurry to follow. Maybe they assumed we were already trapped anyway. Only one day some Czech partisans ran by the MG and paid a high price for their clumsiness.

My last assignment as part of the rear guard, on May 5, 1945, was the most disastrous. In many cases, an overly quiet front proves to be deceptive. We held a small farmhouse on a gentle hill against the oncoming enemy. The Alsatian and I had set up the MG in the attic. The removal of some wooden shingles was enough to clear a reasonable field of fire. A lonesome dispatch rider delivered the brief order to pick up some of our troops coming from further ahead. We were to send them on to the next intersection. Special caution wouldn't be necessary. A fatal mistake, as it turned out later.

I took the first MG shift while the other two settled down on the ground floor. After some time, I recognized some German soldiers through my binoculars. They were stepping out of the forest about 400 meters away. I thought I was safe, especially because of the dispatch rider's report, and I wanted to let the perhaps 100 or 150 men approach. When they were only about 300 meters away from me, I suddenly heard "*Dawai, dawai.*" I looked through the binoculars again and could clearly see German military coats. The distinctive outline of German steel helmets was visible on their heads. However, as the shreds of Russian words and sentences kept coming, I had no doubt left. Russians in German uniforms! A deceitful trick.

I immediately sounded the alarm. Still groggy, the Alsatian knelt behind the MG, looked through the iron sight, and confirmed my observation with a long burst of fire. He did not need a firing command. The sergeant was also on his feet in seconds and fired through the kitchen window. I used the semiautomatic to shoot between the exposed rafters to feign greater numbers. After about half a belt, the MG suddenly jammed. My comrade took it out of the tripod mount and rammed it vertically against the floor. A measure that in most cases solved the problem. However, this time, we had no such luck. The wooden shaft broke so awkwardly that the bottom plate and spring slipped out of their casing. The MG had become unusable, that much was certain. The sergeant realized that we were not firing anymore and ordered our withdrawal. I strapped the MG mount on my back and fired the last of my magazine at the enemy. In the meantime, the Russians had already opened machine-gun fire on the attic, hurrying us up. Behind the house was a slightly rising field that ended in a forest. That was where we had to go. On the ground floor, the sergeant told us we should go out through the main entrance one by one. He would give us covering fire and be the last one to retreat. Just as I was about to leave the house after the Alsatian, a heavy hail of bullets forced me to the ground. I was forced to crawl on. In the middle of the field, I turned around and saw the sergeant as he stood with his MP in the entrance, legs firmly spread in the doorframe, snarling and firing at the Russians.

All around me projectiles hit the ground. That's how close the enemy was. With great luck, I reached a flat furrow not far from the edge of the forest. From there I looked back again. The sergeant had already left the house, but they must have caught him. I only saw how he tried in vain to raise his upper body and repeatedly grabbed his stomach. He gestured to me to continue with a pained face. I can still see it as if it happened yesterday. My last image of him is how he sat up again and sent a long burst of fire to the Russians. Suddenly, his upper body gave way, and he collapsed. Dead. The sound of approaching mortar shells urged me on.

I met the Alsatian in a ravine at the edge of the forest and told him about the fate of our esteemed comrade. Ever since Nikopol, he had saved us a dozen times from sure death. He had always been calm and showed countenance even in hopeless situations. Even after the dramatic loss of his entire family, he did not give up his "lads" but looked after us with educational stringency and paternal care. It was exasperating that disaster always had to claim the best. Those selfless fighters who at all times, in life, in death, in victory or defeat, established the ethos of pure comradeship and genuine soldierhood.

Deeply shocked and heartbroken, we continued on our way back. I had had enough. Enough of the killing. Enough of the dying. In the eyes of the Alsatian I saw a question I was also asking myself. When would this terrible war come to an end, the cannons fall silent, the armories shut down? When would we finally be able to return to life instead of crawling, slaying, and destroying?

CHAPTER 9
WOE TO THE DEFEATED

The last days of the war were marked by total chaos. Everywhere one saw the work of flying court-martials, which carried out their criminal, murderous order with fanatical hatred right up to the last minute. Landser and civilians hanging from trees and telegraph poles. Many with signs around their necks that still cried for the Endsieg. Many of them bloated by the radiance of the spring sun, almost looking like caricatures. There was nothing left that could have shaken me after all the experiences as a frontline soldier. Mine and the Alsatian's only aspiration was to get home. Our final destination after our long and arduous journey.

The two of us had come as far as Olomouc and there we met the remains of various units. Unmanned guns and tracked vehicles were everywhere. Rising soot swirls still testified of the self-destruction order of their former operating crews, which of course was fulfilled. Here we also learned about the fall of Berlin and the suicide of Hitler. The architect of this catastrophe, unprecedented in human history, had shirked his responsibility in one last cowardly act. With his death also the oath to which we as soldiers felt committed died. Messages of the final capitulation of the German Wehrmacht on May 8,

1945, as well as reports of the issued demarcation lines spread like wildfire. The Russians were in Lower Austria, the Americans in Upper Austria. Styria was occupied by the British, although rumors of fighting between Wehrmacht units and the Red Army in the East Styrian borderland made the rounds. Deep in Central Bohemia, the Army Group Center was still surrounded. Almost a million German soldiers, including the bulk of 3 GD. Everyone tried to escape Russian captivity. On their own and alone. Thus, for the two of us, the time had come to go our separate ways. While the Alsatian wanted to march to Bavaria, I made the decision to make my way to the part of Austria occupied by the Western Allies.

So, for the last time, we stood opposite each other by an overgrown pond. Face to face. I had a lump in my throat, as if it were goodbye forever. The Alsatian watched the reeds rhythmically fluctuating in the wind with a sad look on his face. I tried desperately to find the right words, words that would be worthy of a farewell, but could not utter a single syllable. We had escaped death together countless times. Moreover, death had scornfully been defied, and we had survived. The comradely bond that this war had created between us was, in the end, greater than the war itself. For me it had always been a privilege to fight alongside such comrades.

"Hans, is it not about time you chuck that thing away? It has been a burden long enough."

Only then did I realize that I was still carrying the MG mount. Amazed at how used I was to the heavy burden, I shrugged it off and dropped it into the pond.

"Well, Emil, look after yourself. And thank you for everything."

We gripped each other by the shoulder almost at the same time and pressed our palms together firmly.

"And Hans, do not forget what I always told you … carry on and on …"

"I know … until the eyes shut!"

For seconds we were surrounded by a dead silence. Then we turned and disappeared without looking back. Into the adjacent shrubbery.

I headed southwest all day long with a firm stride. At first, attached to a Wehrmacht column, and then, when no progress was possible due to the clogged-up roads, as a lone wanderer across scattered fields and meadows. At night I settled down in a wooded area. I would always search in the undergrowth for places that were hard to reach, places used by wild animals for the same reason. If enemy troops were to comb the forest, I would hear them from afar. That would give me my chance to disappear in the opposite direction of the upthrown dust unnoticed.

The next morning I happened to pass a parked radio car. The radio wires were still attached in a star shape to the surrounding trees. After careful observation, I decided to look for something useful and actually found an oversized map and a compass. According to them, it was about 100 kilometers to the Austrian border. That is, as the crow flies. Searching the radio car further, I found a loaded pistol in the drawer under the radio, which I swapped immediately for my semiautomatic. After all, I wanted to get ahead as fast as possible and only carry the bare necessities. As I walked around the car, I froze when I saw three Landser with their hands tied behind their backs in front of me. Murdered by a shot in the neck. The blood was still fresh. Their murderers had to be close. In addition, one of the victims had an iron cross in his mouth, a disturbing sight. I remembered my own awards and the risk they exposed me to. I sneaked back into the undergrowth and kept my head down for the rest of the day. Close Combat Clasp, Infantry Assault Badge, Iron Cross

2nd Class, and the Wound Badge in Black were unceremoniously removed from my uniform coat and buried at the foot of a burly birch, where they are probably still today. But I could just not part with the tinny Edelweiss on my mountain cap. Maybe it would bring me luck, as it had before.

From then on, I no longer had any illusions of a quick return to my native soil. On the contrary, I decided to march only at dawn and at dusk. Keeping well away from all roads and villages. That was maybe 10 to 15 kilometers a day. In the twilight phases, all life naturally rests, and with eyes used to the dark, I still had good vision. So it went on for a few days until one night in the absence of any alternatives, I had to rest in an overgrown hole in the ground. The surrounding terrain seemed completely open and I was already exhausted. Due to the past strains I unintentionally fell into a deep sleep. Suddenly I heard crackling branches behind me. Before I knew it, a Russian jumped into the hole. I was about to reach for the pistol when I saw his hands up in the air. We stared at each other for what felt like eternity. Shocked and paralyzed by the unreal situation.

It was the Russian who finally interrupted the silence, whispering *"Damoi, damoi,"* which means something like "home." He obviously did not want to hurt me. So I pointed to the direction I came from and said *"Dam"* (there). We both nodded goodbye. Then he disappeared as suddenly as he had arrived. Stunned, I glanced after him. Why hadn't he killed me? Was he a Red Army soldier or perhaps a Russian volunteer pressed into German service? In any case, it would have been easy for him to kill me. But apparently his longing for home was stronger than the simple lust for murder. At that moment, I realized that I shared my wishes and hopes with those on the other side. I too longed for home. All the time. For a short time, the war had shown its human face— even though technically it was already over. The next day, however, when a dozen Landser were chased like hares across some meadow and fell victim to enemy bullets, one thing became very clear to me: the war and the fledgling peace that follows bring out all the excesses of man's worst qualities.

From then on, the increasingly open terrain and the increasing hunger caused me a great deal of anxiety. My rations had been consumed a long time ago. Obtaining something edible meant visiting human settlements. However big the risk, my emaciated body forced me to do something. Love makes blind, as the old saying goes. The same applies for hunger. From my hideout I could clearly see the countless patrols that roamed the hills. In off-road vehicles, on horses, or on foot. Just off a major road lay a lonely farm. That was where I would strike in the early hours of the night. Said and done. I stole toward a wooden shed attached to the courtyard like a cat. The pistol held at my chest ready to fire. Again and again, I stopped and listened out into the night for even the smallest signs of danger. At the wooden door, I moved the heavy bolt to the side with the utmost care. Quietly I pushed the door open and stepped into the room beyond. Ghostly moonlight flooded the ground. Feverishly, my eyes searched for heaps of potatoes, turnips, or anything useful. And then, a suppressed wheeze. Cattle? No! It smelled very different.

Someone pushed up from the floor. He addressed me with a grumpy tone. "*Cos se déje?*" (What's going on?) I panicked and took a step back, only to stumble over an obstacle and crash to the ground. Immediately, all hell broke loose. Screams. Half a dozen figures suddenly rose. Chaotic tumult in the hut. I rolled off. Leaped toward the exit. More screams from the courtyard building. Lights went on. Accompanied by the clanking of guns. While trying to escape I brushed against the door and fell to the floor a second time. Lost the gun and precious seconds. I was not quite across the yard yet when shots passed dangerously close to me. I lay down quickly. Then continued crawling this time. When I wanted to jump up again, I looked straight into a rifle barrel. The end! *"Ty německá prasata."* (You German bastard.)

The figure moved slowly toward me, holding me at gunpoint. More Czechs came running from the back and surrounded me in a semicircle. Lying on the floor, I stretched out my arms to show that I was unarmed. Then I heard steps in the grass close to my hip. A thunderous blow to the back of my head, and I lost consciousness.

My escape had come to an end. I had fallen into the hands of Czech partisans. Still completely stunned by the capture, the very next day I was dragged to a cart, sat up in the back, and taken to the nearby village under heavy guard. There, a whole series of Landser who had a similarly bad fate. At the marketplace, I fell hard on the cobblestones and was driven toward the other prisoners under lashes. I crawled on all fours between protective legs and finally obeyed the order to lift my hands and lean against a wall. We stood there for almost half the day. With pale faces and aching limbs. Surrounded by Czechs drunk on alcohol and victory. People who wanted to let off steam on us godforsaken Landser. But they could not make up their minds whether they should shoot us, beat us to death, or hang us. In the heated debate, even more Czechs entered the brawl. An adolescent Czech, drunk out of his mind and hung with cartridges, went through the line again and again. Each time he held a pistol to our heads. Muttering devilish curses, he waited until the maltreated creature in front of him began to tremble. Then he would squeeze the trigger. *Click!* Nothing. Then he pulled the pistol cock back and moved on to his next victim. Under the roaring applause of the rabble, who at no time in human history have missed an opportunity to latch on to the victor's boots, to judge where there was nothing to judge. After a short while, it started to stink of urine and feces. I too had shat my pants.

When we were finally assembled into a small marching column and moved to the next village, the spectacle was repeated. We were beaten and abused at every opportunity. Everyone joined in. The young, the old, men and women. German soldiers lay by the side of the road. Shot, stabbed. "Vae victis," woe to the vanquished, was the motto of the new-born peace. Many Landser wished for a return of the war—at least they would have had part of their fate in their own hands. Here, however, one was at the mercy of the most despicable actions of the angry populace. Only an incoming Russian patrol ended the humiliation by the Czechs. We were arrested and taken to an ad hoc collection camp at the foot of a castle. Although already mid-May, the nights were still cold. On top of that, the partisans had taken all our kit when they had captured us. Lucky he who still had a pair of shoes and his uniform. Wedding rings, watches, and family photos had also fallen victim to the blind robbery. As had forks and spoons. The bad treatment of the first few days after my capture had severely damaged my health. My whole body was covered in bruises and minor wounds. Add that to constantly lying on the cold ground and the lack of nourishment, and my condition was worsening rapidly. I got a fever. It took a few days until the first meal was finally served. But to receive this, you had to take the very steep climb up to the castle and join a long queue.

I was already too exhausted for that. Once again, our good comradeship was a savior in the hour of need. A Jäger, one I knew from the retreat battles, fed me, often sharing his meager meal with me. After a few days, I had recovered enough to manage the walk to the castle.

After another week they began to clear the camp. They took us to the provincial train station, where they penned us into cattle cars, forty in each, and transported us south. Some Austrian town signs were spotted, and very briefly the hope of a speedy return to our homeland flickered up. But in the end, we moved further and further away from our homeland and then drove into Budapest. In Romania, we switched from narrow-gauge to wide-gauge railways, and by now even the last of the optimists knew what had hit us. Years of imprisonment in the deep heart of Russia lay ahead of us. And for quite a few, this would be their very last journey. At the time, I was almost twenty.

The journey in the cattle car took a total of four weeks. The amenities were spartan. No straw, no stove, only the hard wooden floor, in the middle of which there was a small hole for relief. The two small windows were blocked with barbed wire and the door was closed with a thick iron lock. We slept in turns. Two-thirds of the POWs standing against the walls, the rest sleeping in the middle. It took several days before the first meal was put in front of us. We had already arrived in the east of Hungary when they finally gave us cabbage soup. Then, in Ukraine, we stood around in a freight yard for days on end. Here we learned of our fate for the first time. The guards told us that we were to be brought to an arms factory near the Volga. What also became apparent was the chronic food shortage of the Red Army. The guards were not much better off than us. They also often went days without food.

Screaming to a halt, the train finally stopped in the mighty Central Russian industrial city of Gorki. You could see the massive blast furnaces from a distance. Here, at the confluence of the rivers Oka and Volga, the Communist regime had built huge armament centers during the last decades. Hundreds of tanks and thousands of trucks were rolled out of the massive factory halls every month. The whole city was constantly awake. After the end of the war, several large prisoner-of-war camps had been built all around. They were in desperate need of workers. First of all, the beleaguered Soviet Empire had to be rebuilt and, secondly, the big arms race with the Western Allies was already kicking off. After the delousing, the shaving of the heads, and the loss of the last of our belongings, we moved into our new home. You have to have a strong sense of irony to be able to call the barracks where we vegetated a home. The walls were made of wood and the wind was constantly whistling through the unevenly planed boards. This should prove to be difficult for us, especially during the winter months. The heating made no difference at all and was a useless effort at the same time. To the left and right of the walls, the Russian builders had installed three-story wooden cots. During the first months of captivity, there was so little space that even the passages in between were fully occupied.

It was only after many a Landser had died of either illness or exhaustion that the space problem "improved." Outside the barracks there was a large roll-call square. There we had to assemble every day at half past five for counting. Afterward we marched in work columns to our jobs a fair few kilometers away. Work was done seven days a week—except for one day at Christmas and Easter—all year round.

My task force, also called a brigade, was initially responsible for filling the blast furnaces. It was our task to supply different crude ores, scrap metals, and coal to the chute in a wheelbarrow, and then shovel it in. The climbs and the heavy loads turned this into agonizing work. You could not rest because a minimum quota had to be fulfilled every day. If you didn't reach it, your food ration was reduced. This, in turn, weakened the emaciated body even more, and usually led to death. Luckily there were a lot of hard-working people in my group who were doing well. We worked on the principle of divided labor. This way, we soon succeeded in exceeding the norm. The result was special portions during food distribution, which we also needed urgently. Nevertheless, things were "arranged" at every opportunity. At that time, it was a famous term for all activities related to the improvised procurement of food, clothing, or other necessities. We arranged a lot when we had to unload the barges on the Volga. Despite the threat of draconian punishment. When unsupervised, we stole away like magpies.

One of those days has remained a special memory. A ship loaded with potatoes had just docked and had to be unloaded at night. Armed with baskets and sacks, we had to bring the cargo into a potato bunker. While I was swinging back and forth between the ship and the warehouse, at irregular intervals I let a single potato roll down the side of a drainage pit. After we finished, I grabbed a sack, put my loot in, and stashed it under my padded jacket. With the impending feast in mind, I made my way back to the camp, and was promptly stopped by a young officer. Of course, he immediately discovered the bulge on my stomach, took the bag from me, and slapped me. He ordered me to report the next morning to receive my punishment. I remembered a similar incident on the Drava bridge during my training, and of course, I did not dream of following the order. So, the next morning, I kept quiet as the raging officer crossed the ranks and searched for me. He probably had not been able to recognize my face in the gathering darkness, and so I got away with it.

The months passed and winter approached. The terrible Russian cold and the icy easterly wind can only be felt by those who have experienced it. Words cannot describe the terrible months of freezing cold. It has to be said that my Blast Furnace Work Commando was still getting away lightly. It was warmer close to the stoves. By contrast, the bloodletting of the Wood Commando, which went to the woods every day to cut down trees, was enormous. The life of many a comrade ended in this frozen hell. It became a regular occurrence for me to find one of my neighbors frozen stiff in the mornings. The dead were taken out of the barracks every morning, put on a wagon, and driven to a canyon, where they found their final resting place. Without prayer, without a cross to mark the grave. I was assigned to the Funeral Commando several times, too. A comrade from Salzburg, who had been lying on a bunk close to me a few days before, lay awkwardly squished beneath a layer of frozen dead. As I gradually shoveled the slag brought in from the furnaces across his body, descriptions of his two angelic daughters came to my mind. Private details that he sometimes entrusted to me before falling asleep. I cried without shedding a tear. It was much too cold at -30 °C. That was the bitter plight of Russian captives.

With the return of the spring sun, a new zest for life unfolded in us emaciated figures. 1946 was also the year when we were increasingly dispatched to the surrounding areas of Gorki. Here our main purpose was to help manage the collective farms. What still stumps me today is that the Russians' approach to agriculture and animal husbandry was so old-fashioned. One of the main reasons for this was certainly the political system which did not allow efficiency. The levies for the collective were too high and the farmers were not allowed to keep enough of the harvest. Additional efforts in the field meant more taxes, which was not exactly motivating. No wonder that the huge Soviet Empire was constantly suffering from food shortages. Our Russian guards often got less food than us prisoners of war. They had probably imagined a different life after the war. Somehow it seemed to me that there were only losers among us ordinary soldiers. The laurels and fruits of victory had apparently been divided within other classes of society.

When we were further away from the main camp, we would sleep at the collective farms. Of course with more or less the same lack of comfort, but without the barbed wire. I have differing memories of the Russian population as far as the behavior toward us prisoners is concerned. There were farmers with whom we sat at the same table and shared their scanty food. Then there were those tyrants who did not care for our lives. Personally, in all this time, I never came to understand our "host nation." The successful exploration of the Russian soul was denied to me. An experience in August 1946 is indicative of this.

I had been staying with a Russian peasant family in the suburbs of Gorki and had helped with various jobs. Since I proved to be a lot more skillful in dealing with the plow than the Russians themselves, I enjoyed something like respect. Accordingly, the treatment in this house was good, and they maintained an almost friendly relationship with me. One day the farmer's wife told me to take the tram out of town to collect some nettles.

I took a basket and made my way to the forest and found a few smaller nettle fields which I began to pick immediately. Suddenly an elderly Russian came running toward me with an iron rod in his hand. Before I could even justify myself, the first blow had hit me directly on the head. I instinctively jerked my hands up to protect myself and rushed forward to move myself out of the immediate danger area. But for no apparent reason he ran after me and, cursing loudly, continued to hit my head and chest. I could already feel the blood streaming down my cheeks and my legs began to weaken. If I did not succeed to escape from this madman soon, he would kill me. To fight back and possibly hurt a Russian, on the other hand, would have had some serious consequences for me. Justice was not necessarily in favor of prisoners during those years.

With reeling senses and summoning my last ounces of strength I reached a small peasant hut, where I immediately banged my fist violently against the door. An elderly lady opened and saw what was going on. She confronted the

Russian who had been following me with a raised voice and finally brought about his withdrawal. I stood there with weak knees and a bleeding head wound. But instead of helping me, the old Russian lady slammed the door in my face and left me standing in the rain.

As if in a trance, I stumbled back to the tram stop and rode the tram back to my farmer family. Hundreds of people saw me on the way, but none of them made serious attempts to help me. On the contrary, they avoided me like the plague and remained at a distance despite the overcrowded carriage. What did the life of a German prisoner of war mean to this victorious power anyway? I had to serve as her slave, and if I died, so be it. My shirt was soaked with blood and a light crust had already formed on my shaven head. So I went back to my starting point. The mistress of the house immediately clapped her hands over her head and let out a deep sigh. With tears in her eyes supporting my already collapsing body, she led me into the kitchen. Her sitting me down on a chair is the last thing I remember. After that, total darkness came over me.

I woke up days later at Gorki City Hospital. Wrapped in white sheets and lying on a real bed, I felt like I was on another planet. All around me were sick Russians who sized me up with evil eyes. The arrival of a doctor interrupted the unpleasant atmosphere. She only checked my pulse, the bandage, and my temperature, and without saying a word she turned to the next patient. This went on for a few days until I finally got a visit from the farmer's wife. I could tell immediately from her face that she was genuinely glad to see me again. She then told me what had happened to me after she had dragged me into the kitchen. Three years of Russia also had a positive effect on my Russian proficiency, and so I was able to follow her easily. According to her descriptions, she and her husband rode me to the hospital in a cart. Fortunately, they managed to get me admitted for medical treatment. Although my injuries were quickly cleaned and stitched up, I developed a high fever a short time later. At first, there was little optimism that the high temperature could be brought under control. My body was already too weak. After a few days, when the farmer's wife came to see me regularly and sat by my side, my condition improved noticeably. Thank God that my inner spirit was not completely extinguished.

Apart from my head wound, pretty much my entire upper body was covered in bruises. The old Russian had done a stern job with his iron rod and had put me in a bad way. On the other hand, there was the Russian peasant woman without whose help I certainly would not have survived. There are good and bad people. In every country. That was perhaps the most important realization of my unhappy time in captivity. Of course, my "cushy patient's life" did not last long. After a medical commission had decided I was fit for work, it was back to the armory with me. Retrospectively, this short break had done me good. My weight and soul had recovered a bit, and I looked to the future with confidence. Once back at the factory and up until my release, I went through all levels of tank production. From welding the hull to setting up the turret to spraying camouflage paint. There was hardly any work in the production cycle of the T-34 tank that I did not do.

In early 1947, a few improvements finally took hold in our POW lives. New padded jackets and straw-filled blankets were issued. The food was still sparse and unvaried. During this time, I was also allowed to write my first letter home. The post was handled via the Red Cross. This supranational and impartial organization was respected, or at least tolerated, even here in Mother Russia. A total of twenty-five words were allowed on a plain postcard. Yes, not a word more! The content, of course, was subject to censorship. Woe to the one who wrote something derogatory about the Soviet Union or his imprisonment. For that, you would end up in something like solitary confinement and could forget about going home. At any rate, I chose my words carefully. "Dear family! I am fine. I am healthy. I'm sure I'll be home soon …" or something to that effect. As a matter of fact, I learned later on that this had been my first sign of life to my loved ones in almost two years. In the last months of the war, all traces of me had been lost. My father, after feverish investigations, was bluntly told that I had been reported dead. According to the information he received, Czech partisans had shot me near Brno. This message was not corrected until 1947, when it became apparent that I was still alive.

Like every part of life, my time as a POW eventually came to an end. Homecoming rumors became more common during the summer of 1947, and there were already some early departures from the camp. The Russians were adept at keeping us busy with deliberately spread rumors. One time, it was said that only the Austrians could go home, another time a complete halt to all releases was announced. It took no small amount of inner strength to not let oneself be worn down by these recurring disappointments. Patience was the virtue of the hour. At some point, it would be rewarded. We all hoped for that. Until that moment came, it was important to stay healthy and carry on. Too big was the longing for the East Styrian hills I call my home.

CHAPTER 10
THE END OF THE BEGINNING

The first snow had already fallen in these inhospitable Russian expanses. Another winter, my fifth in Russia, had arrived. It was to be my last. At the end of November 1947, there was suddenly a great deal of excitement in the camp. A load of reasonably usable winter clothes had arrived. We, the prisoners of war, were to be newly kitted out and then to return home. Most of us were rather skeptical about what had happened. There had been similar announcements in the past. German prisoners of war were fed a bit more for a while, provided with new clothes, and then just put in front of Soviet cameras. The propaganda material thus obtained was sold to the West as proof of the hospitality of the Russian Bear. Once the cameras were gone, the poor Landser were back again in their tattered cotton jackets. I experienced this foul play twice.

But this time, my skepticism proved inappropriate. After a last delousing and after being handed back our dirty worn work clothes, we were marched in column to the station. We passed by the Russian guards, and they walked us over a paved road built by the Landser and into an industrial quarter. There, several hundred Austrians boarded the waiting freight wagons. Once the train moved out, we secretly held back our joy. After all, we did not want to upset the Russians. The further the train rolled west, the lighter the mood became. Via Moscow the route led to South Ukraine. Passing Odessa to the north, we arrived in Romania, and later in Hungary. Almost the same way that I had put under my soles during the retreat of 1943–44. The transport often stopped for long periods of time to give way to other trains.

When we finally crossed the new Austrian border and drove into Wiener Neustadt, the feeling was unprecedented. A huge crowd was waiting for us home-comers. You could see many tears of joy but also many disappointed faces. Almost every second, relatives asked about the whereabouts of family members. Many a lovely little child stood on the platform with a sign with a photo of their missing father in their small hands. A heartbreaking sight. Unfortunately, only in the rarest of cases one of us returnees could give the wanted information.

They served us a nutritious meal and we received 50 shillings each. After hours of waiting, I took the next train to Graz, and from there the bus to Fürstenfeld. Together with some comrades, I reached my home district around noon on Christmas Eve of 1947. The last kilometers from the train station to the family farm were to be covered on foot. I fell into my marching step and entered the last stage of my long journey.

With every meter, my heart pounded louder and louder. Could it be true? Was I really back on my native soil after surviving five years of martyrdom? The sight of my sister Johanna, who had learned of my arrival by phone and had come out to meet me on the dirt track, wiped my thoughts away. Overjoyed at the reunion, we fell into each other's arms. The last stretch of road flew like clouds.

Much had changed during my absence. The death of my mother and many relatives and friends weighed heavy on me. It took me a long time to get used to my homeland again. The softly sprung bed, the regular meals, the warm room, and especially the company of my loved ones were alien to me at first. The prudent nature of my father helped me a lot with my reintegration into civilian life. He was so overjoyed to see me alive that he burst into tears. It was the only time I ever saw him like this. In addition to my soul, my body also showed unusual reactions. In the weeks after returning home, I gained weight on an almost daily basis. As a physical response to the years of starvation, my organism stored every calorie it could get. At the height of it all I weighed a good 85 kilograms. And that for a young man who stood at a height of under 170 centimeters.

When I went to my hometown's first festival months after, I barely recognized any of the young people around me. The hustle and bustle told me that the past had been left behind long ago. It was like there had never been a war. In a frontline soldier, however, the memories of the struggle and deprivations live on relentlessly. Death, with its insatiable hunger for the living, had become a matter of course. How should you handle it? Who would understand? There was no room for weakness in these difficult days of the dawning second half of the twentieth century. Reconstruction called for every helping hand. The war experiences had to be pushed aside. But would that be so easy?

I stood with my father on the steep slopes of the parental farm and held a scythe in my hand. He had just stuffed his pipe, and he blew the smoke into the air. With expertise, he scanned the slope. The grass was green as ever. The smell of harvest was in the air.

"Over there, that's where we start. The grass is already tall there."

I paused for a moment and saw in my mind the sergeant with the MP standing in the doorway.

"Yes father, you are right!"

"Let us start …"

Hans Kahr (left) with his father (right). Haymaking in the early '50s.

EPILOGUE

It is immensely difficult to draw a chronologically flawless picture of one's own war experiences when they are half a century back. The reader may, therefore, forgive us for any inaccuracies in time and location. Unless clearly anchored in my notes or memories, they either had to be taken from relevant literature or archives or clarified in conversations with surviving veterans of the 3rd Gebirgsjäger Division.

As for the events themselves, they are authentic and a testimony to the terrible effects that war has on people. If you have grown up in peace, prosperity, and stable political conditions, then you should judge World War II veterans wisely. The difference between an ideal world and the blood-smeared reality of war is huge. This gap cannot be closed by a book, a film, or a well-researched documentation of goings-on in the world. Only those who really experienced the war will want to preserve peace with all their might.

You, the reader, may wonder what happened to me and the other people mentioned after the war. Well, in the end, I took over my parents' farm and started a family, just as it was intended when I was born. Working in nature and with the animals was my lifelong passion. As expected, I found solid support among the mountain people, within my family, in faith, and in the village community. My schoolmate and

Until the Eyes Shut

comrade Toni did not return from Russian captivity until 1949. Heavily marked but still alive. He also took over his father's farm and remained a farmer all his life. In him, I had someone with whom I could talk openly about the war. In hindsight, these conversations helped us a lot in processing the many traumatic experiences we endured.

And the Alsatian? Unfortunately, all traces of him were lost in the chaos of the last days of war. Did he get through it? I sincerely hope so. Without him, I would not have been able to write these lines today. He saved my life countless times.

Lost in thought, my gaze wanders out to the kitchen window edged with frost flowers. There is a storm outside, and snow. The landscape is covered by a white-grey curtain, as it had been in February 1944.

Suddenly a figure emerges from the snow. It seems to beckon me. I hear a soft but familiar voice: "Come on, Hans, come ... We are waiting for you."

I close my eyes ...

and let go ...

Made in the USA
Las Vegas, NV
08 June 2021